The Pickleball Advantage: How America's Fastest-Growing Sport Builds Your Body, Brain, and Network

From Stress Relief to Strategic Networking—Why CEOs, Entrepreneurs, and High Achievers Are Picking Up the Paddle

Dr. Ben Chuba
&
Nicci Brochard

The Pickleball Advantage: How America's Fastest-Growing Sport Builds Your Body, Brain, and Network

From Stress Relief to Strategic Networking—Why CEOs, Entrepreneurs, and High Achievers Are Picking Up the Paddle

CROSSBORDER

New York, London, Quebec

Contents

Introduction

Pickleball has quietly staged a revolution. Once seen as a quirky backyard pastime, it has surged to become the fastest-growing sport in America, attracting millions of new players every year. But its real story isn't just about paddles, nets, and courts—it's about the unexpected ways this game is reshaping health, focus, and professional success.

For busy executives, entrepreneurs, and high achievers, the challenge of staying fit, sharp, and socially connected often competes with endless deadlines and demanding schedules. Golf once held the crown as the sport of business, but five-hour rounds feel impossible in a calendar already bursting with meetings. Pickleball, by contrast, delivers a high-energy, social, and strategic experience in under an hour—making it the perfect fit for professionals who want maximum return on their time investment.

On the court, the benefits are immediate: a full-body workout, a mental reset from stress, and the spark of friendly competition. Beyond the court, the ripple effect is even more powerful. Deals are struck between volleys. Partnerships are born during doubles play. Friendships deepen over post-game laughter. The sport blends physical wellness, mental agility, and networking opportunities in a way that few activities ever could.

This book unpacks why high performers across industries are trading briefcases for paddles and discovering advantages that extend far beyond fitness. Through stories, data, and strategy, it explores how pickleball strengthens not just the body, but also the brain and professional network.

Pickleball isn't a passing trend. It's a cultural movement with lasting impact. And for those ready to embrace it, the rewards—personal, professional, and social—are only just beginning. The paddle, quite literally, is in your hands.

Nicci and I (Ben) thank you immensely for choosing our book. We promise you a great time ahead.

Chapter 1

The Pickleball Phenomenon –
America's Fastest-Growing Sport

U.S. pickleball participation has skyrocketed in recent years, reaching 19.8 million players in 2024 – a 45.8% increase from 2023 and an astounding 311% growth over the past three years. The sport's meteoric rise has earned it the title of America's fastest-growing sport for four years running.

Pickleball has rapidly evolved from a quirky niche pastime to a national phenomenon. In parks, gymnasiums, and even corporate campuses across the country, the "pop" of a pickleball echoes daily as millions pick up paddles. The growth has been nothing short of explosive: an estimated 19.8 million Americans played pickleball in 2024, up nearly 46% from the prior year. In fact, pickleball participation has surged 311% over the last three years, cementing its status as *the fastest-growing sport in the United States for the fourth consecutive year.* This unprecedented boom is drawing players across all ages and backgrounds, and it's especially capturing the attention of busy professionals and executives. What was once an obscure game with a funny name is now a cultural craze – and it shows no signs of being a passing fad. In this chapter, we explore the factors behind pickleball's meteoric rise and why high-achievers in business are embracing the paddle with enthusiasm.

1.1 From Obscurity to Mainstream: A Rapid Rise

Just a decade ago, few people had even heard of pickleball; today it's a fixture of American recreation. The sport was invented in 1965 on Bainbridge Island, Washington, but for most of its history it remained a small, regional pastime. Even Bill Gates – who grew up playing pickleball in the 1970s after his father built a court at their Seattle home – recalled that *"at the time, the pickleball community was very small. I doubt there were more than a thousand people in the Seattle area who had ever seen the sport… And I don't think anyone expected it would ever become a national phenomenon."* Pickleball indeed languished in obscurity for decades, played primarily in retirement communities and YMCAs. But as the 2010s progressed, a few converging forces sent the sport's popularity soaring into the mainstream.

Media exposure and cultural buzz played a key role in legitimizing pickleball. Gates himself realized the game had *"gotten serious"* when even the buttoned-down *Economist* ran a story on pickleball's newfound fame. By the early 2020s, pickleball segments were popping up on morning news shows and in major newspapers. In late 2022, CBS aired a star-studded prime-time special called "Pickled" – a comic pickleball tournament hosted by Stephen Colbert featuring celebrities from Paul Rudd to Serena Williams competing on the court for charity. The mere existence of a televised celebrity pickleball event underscored how far into the mainstream the sport had leapt. What once might have been dismissed as a quirky fad was now firmly entrenched in popular culture.

Beyond media coverage, the numbers themselves demanded attention. In 2022 and 2023, pickleball's U.S. participation exploded at a rate unheard of in sports. According to the Sports & Fitness Industry Association, participation jumped 85.7% in 2022, then another 51.8% from 2022 to 2023– growth rates that *far outpaced every other sport in America.* Pickleball wasn't just growing; it was *breaking records.* By early 2024, the SFIA declared for the fourth year in a row that pickleball had the fastest-growing participation of any sport, easily eclipsing gains seen in running, basketball, and other popular activities. Key milestones marked its ascent from obscurity: in 2021, USA Pickleball (the national governing body) registered its 50,000th member; in 2022, the sport's first professional tours were formed; and by 2023, local governments nationwide were repurposing underused tennis courts en masse to meet demand for pickleball play. What had started as a quiet community game had transformed into a full-blown movement.

Several factors converged to catapult pickleball into the mainstream. First, the game itself proved to be incredibly accessible (more on that in the next section), which lowered barriers to adoption. Second, the onset of the COVID-19 pandemic in 2020 created a unique opportunity for outdoor sports. With gyms closed and many team sports on hiatus, Americans desperately sought safe, distanced ways to stay active. Pickleball, with its small courts and natural spacing, emerged as an ideal pandemic pastime. *"As the virus spread and prevented people from playing traditional team sports, pickleball was seen as a safe, socially distant way to be outdoors and stay active,"* one report noted. Local parks that remained open saw surges of new players trying the game, often chalking pickleball lines on empty parking lots or temporarily lowering badminton nets in driveways. Entire neighborhoods discovered pickleball as a lifeline for exercise and social connection during lockdowns. *"Back then, they opened the gates for us during COVID… we just played as much as we could to be outside and play safely with our family,"* recalled one parks association president, describing how her San Antonio community's pickleball habit began. This pandemic boost gave pickleball a massive jolt of momentum precisely at a time when many other sports were stalled.

Another catalyst was the sport's sheer fun and simplicity – a quality that turned curious first-timers into passionate regulars. Pickleball has a lighthearted spirit (even its terminology, from the "kitchen" to the "dink," is endearingly quirky) coupled with a competitive edge that keeps players coming back. Games are quick, typically 10–15 minutes, delivering bursts of excitement without requiring an all-day commitment. Equipment is minimal and inexpensive – just a paddle and a plastic ball – meaning anyone can play without a major investment. The rules are simple enough to learn in a single session, yet the strategies can scale up in complexity for advanced players. This mix of *"easy to learn, hard to master"* makes pickleball addictive. *"The best thing about pickleball, however, is that it's just super fun,"* Gates says from decades of experience, noting that he still plays weekly with friends and family. That pure enjoyability translated into word-of-mouth buzz. Friends dragged friends out to try the game; grandparents taught grandkids; coworkers set up lunchtime matches in parking lots. The *social contagion* of pickleball – its ability to "hook" newcomers almost instantly – fueled exponential growth at the grassroots level.

By the mid-2020s, the result of these converging forces was undeniable: pickleball became a cultural craze. It is now common to see public parks with dozens of pickleball courts packed morning to night, paddles stacked along fences as players line up for their turn. Municipalities have scrambled to convert tennis courts or build new pickleball facilities, yet demand still outstrips supply in many areas. The sport's infrastructure grew 55% in 2024 alone (over 16,000 places to play nationwide), but even that hasn't fully kept pace with the player boom. On social media, pickleball content is everywhere – highlight clips, comedy skits, and tips – attracting millions of views and new fans (one spectacular rally captured at a pro event amassed over 100 million views online, introducing the sport to countless people who'd never heard of it before). Far from fading, the craze is intensifying. As Tom Cove, president of the SFIA, put it: *"The pickleball craze is alive and well, still the fastest-growing sport in the United States."* Indeed, pickleball has transitioned from novelty to establishment. It's *in* the mainstream now – and as the next sections will show, one reason it's here to stay is that it truly is a sport for everyone.

1.2 A Sport for All Ages and Skill Levels

One of the greatest strengths of pickleball – and a key driver of its broad appeal – is that anyone can play and enjoy it, from young children to senior citizens, from total beginners to seasoned athletes. The game's inclusive design and gentle learning curve make it *"easy to learn, and people of all ages and skill levels can play it"*, as one pickleball club puts it. In an era where many sports struggle to bridge generational or ability gaps, pickleball stands out as genuinely *cross-generational and beginner-friendly*. This section explores how the sport's accessibility has created a community where a 70-year-old retiree can happily rally with a 17-year-old student – and both walk away grinning.

Consider the demographics: while pickleball initially gained traction in senior communities, its player base has dramatically diversified. The average player age has been dropping each year – now sitting in the mid-30s (around 34.8 years old on average by one measure) – even as older adults continue to participate in huge numbers. In fact, recent statistics show that players age 25–34 now form the single largest age bracket in the sport, accounting for about 16.7% of all participants, with the 65+ group close behind at 15.4%. Hot on their heels are college-aged players 18–24 (roughly 13% of players) and an explosion of kids and teens picking up paddles – over 1 million new players under 18 joined in 2023 alone. This is a remarkable age distribution for a sport: essentially a *bell curve spanning from grade-schoolers to grandparents*. Pickleball has managed to attract younger generations in droves while *retaining its older core* – a testament to its multigenerational charm.

What makes pickleball so accessible across ages and skill levels? Several of its fundamental traits lower the barrier to entry compared to other sports:

- **Simple rules and small court**: The basics of pickleball can be learned in minutes. New players often grasp the essential rules – how to serve underhand, when to let the ball bounce, where the "kitchen" no-volley zone is – in their first session. The court is just 20x44 feet (about a third the size of a tennis court), so there's far less ground to cover. This smaller court levels the playing field between the quick and the not-so-quick. A younger player's speed advantage is muted, and an older player's savvy positioning can compensate – making it fun for mixed ages to play together without anyone feeling outmatched by sheer physicality.

- **Slower ball and forgiving pace**: Pickleball uses a lightweight plastic ball (similar to a whiffle ball) that travels significantly slower than a tennis ball. Even when smacked hard, a pickleball has a limited top speed and tends to float more, giving players extra time to react. As Bill Gates describes, *"it doesn't move as fast as a tennis ball… It doesn't take much skill to hit the ball."* For novices or those with limited mobility, this is inviting – you can get rallies going without needing lightning reflexes. Longtime tennis coach and pickleball convert Cindy Bennet notes that in pickleball *"the ball stays in play longer, so beginners get more chances to hit and learn"*, whereas in tennis a newcomer might swing and miss frequently. The slower pace also reduces impact on joints, making it approachable for seniors or people rehabbing injuries.

- **Easy on the body**: Pickleball is relatively low-impact. There's no aggressive running or high jumping required; doubles (the most popular form) involves quick side-to-side shuffles and dinks at the net more than sprints. The underhand serve and no-volley zone mitigate overhead smashing and extreme strain on shoulders or knees. Many older players find they can play pickleball for hours without the aches that a game of basketball or a long run might induce. This has opened the sport to people who thought their competitive athletic days were behind them. It's common to see *"active agers"* in their 60s, 70s, even 80s, dominating a pickleball match with placement and touch, delighting in a sport that keeps them moving without punishing their bodies.

- **Social and cooperative learning**: Pickleball culture is famously welcoming. Experienced players are often eager to help rookies learn the ropes – after all, every pickleball addict remembers that someone introduced *them* to the game not long ago. It's not unusual for a first-timer to show up at a public court and immediately be invited into a doubles game with more seasoned players. Because doubles requires communication and strategy, beginners can effectively partner with veterans and enjoy rallies together. As one industry report highlighted, *"pickleball is one of the few sports where beginners can play alongside experienced players, making it a socially engaging and inclusive activity."* The upshot is a sport where families can play as teams (parents with kids, grandparents with grandkids), and coworkers of varying skill levels can share the court. Everyone improves together, and everyone has fun – no one is left on the sidelines.

The stories emerging from pickleball's rise underscore this universal appeal. In Phoenix, Arizona, a 12-year-old girl teams up with a 72-year-old retired gentleman at a community center tournament – and they bond over their shared love of the game despite the age gap. In Florida, a former college basketball player brings his mother (a non-athlete) out to play, and within weeks she's beating him in doubles thanks to a crafty soft game. High school tennis players are crossing over into pickleball to enjoy a sport they can play casually with relatives and neighbors of any age. And in perhaps the most symbolic image of pickleball's inclusivity, many parks host mornings where *three generations* of a family might occupy one court: grandpa at the net, mom dinking crosscourt, and the teenage kids leaping for smashes – all laughing together. Few sports can boast such a scene.

It helps, too, that pickleball is affordable and logistically easy. A starter paddle-and-ball set can be had for under $40, and since the courts are small, many towns are adding multiple pickleball courts in spaces that might hold only one tennis court. The result is abundant local access – you don't need an expensive country club membership or elaborate gear to join in. This democratization has further broadened the player base. *"Pickleball is more affordable than sports like tennis or golf… and there's no need to be part of a fancy country club,"* one article noted, emphasizing that a decent paddle can cost well under $200 and public courts are often free. In other words, pickleball invites everyone: all ages, all income levels, men and women alike (the gender split is roughly 60/40 male-female, and women's participation is rising each year). A newcomer can literally show up in sneakers, borrow a paddle from a friendly stranger, and be playing within minutes – and that newcomer might be *14 or 74 years old.*

This cross-generational, accessible nature of pickleball has been pivotal in its rapid growth. The sport has effectively *enlarged the tent* of who counts as an "athlete." It appeals to the kid who finds Little League too slow, the 30-something professional who doesn't have time for a 4-hour golf round, and the retiree seeking low-impact exercise and social connection. Busy adults in their 40s can use pickleball as a quick fitness fix or stress reliever, while also playing side by side with their children or aging parents. Inclusivity is baked into pickleball's DNA, and it has paid off richly in participation. As we'll see later in the book, this "sport for everyone" ethos also creates unique networking opportunities – a fact not lost on many business leaders who have joined the pickleball bandwagon. For now, it's enough to recognize that much of pickleball's magic lies in its ability to make *any* newcomer feel, "Hey, I can do this!" – and to have them smiling and sweating with others in no time.

1.3 Why Now? Cultural Shifts and Pandemic Effects

It's worth asking: why did pickleball's boom happen in the past few years, rather than a decade earlier (or later)? The sport has been around since the 1960s, and its core appeal isn't brand new – so what set the stage for the *2020s pickleball explosion*? The answer lies in a perfect storm of cultural shifts and circumstances, from the COVID-19 pandemic to changing leisure trends and a dash of social media virality. This section examines the "why now" – the timely factors that converged to make pickleball the right sport at the right time.

The COVID-19 pandemic is an undeniable accelerant of pickleball's recent growth. When the pandemic hit in 2020, people's recreation habits were upended overnight. Gyms, fitness classes, and indoor sports leagues shut down. Many traditional team sports (like basketball or soccer) were deemed too high-contact or were prohibited due to social distancing measures. Isolated at home, Americans yearned for safe ways to exercise and socialize. Enter pickleball. With its open-air play, natural spacing between players, and minimal physical contact, pickleball emerged as an ideal socially-distanced activity. Neighborhood driveways, cul-de-sacs, and local parks became makeshift pickleball courts as families and teams sought respite from lockdown boredom. Anecdotally, sales of portable pickleball nets and starter paddle sets skyrocketed in mid-2020 as first-timers gave the game a try in their driveways.

The data backs up these stories: one industry white paper noted that *since the pandemic, the pickleball sports industry has witnessed a massive upsurge.* Players themselves often cite the pandemic as their origin story. Jaime Rowan, a player in San Antonio, discovered pickleball during COVID when local courts opened with limited hours for socially distanced play. *"We just played as much as we could to be outside and play safely with our family members. That's kind of how it got started,"* another community player explained of her pickleball group's beginnings in 2020. By allowing people to be active, competitive, and social *while remaining safely apart,* pickleball filled a crucial void. It's no coincidence that in 2021, as pandemic restrictions eased, pickleball's participation absolutely ballooned – many of those who picked it up in 2020 were now utterly hooked and recruiting others. COVID-19, in essence, *accelerated adoption* of a sport that was primed to grow, acting as a catalyst that turned a simmering trend into an explosive phenomenon.

Another factor in the "why now" is a broader shift in how people (especially younger generations and busy adults) choose to spend their leisure time. There's evidence that participation in some traditional sports has been stagnating or declining, particularly among youth. Rigid, time-intensive organized sports leagues have seen dropout rates climb; for instance, surveys show many teens quitting sports by age 15 due to burnout or competing interests. At the same time, fitness trends have been favoring more casual, social, and time-flexible activities. Pickleball fits perfectly into this niche. It offers the competition and camaraderie of a sport without the heavy burdens of time and training that, say, golf or marathon running demand. A pickleball match can be squeezed into a lunch break or played after dinner – it's a *bite-sized sports experience* that appeals to time-crunched professionals and students alike.

Importantly, pickleball also arrived as an *answer to the loneliness and fragmentation of the digital age*. In a time when many were turning to screens for entertainment, pickleball got people outdoors and interacting face-to-face (albeit often six feet apart during COVID). Communities embraced it as a way to rebuild social ties. Neighbors who'd never met started chatting over pickleball games. Recreation centers reported that pickleball was drawing in demographics that typically struggle to find community – from recent empty-nesters to young professionals new in town. The sport's doubles format (typically two teams of two) naturally fosters conversation and teamwork, filling a social wellness need that became especially apparent during pandemic isolation.

Then there's the role of social media and celebrity influence in turbocharging pickleball's popularity in the past couple of years. Pickleball is an inherently *spectator-friendly* game – it's easy to understand even if you've never played, points are quick and often highlight-reel worthy, and the quirky culture (special shots called "opa!" or the "Erne") makes for shareable content. During the pandemic and after, short video clips of incredible pickleball rallies or funny mishaps started going viral on TikTok, Instagram, and YouTube. One now-famous rally from a pro match in 2023 – a mesmerizing 28-shot exchange featuring dives and around-the-post shots – garnered over 100 million views on Instagram, *"served [by] the algorithm to millions who likely hadn't even heard of pickleball. Now, at least some of them are hooked,"* wrote one pickleball media outlet. Those kinds of viral moments introduced the sport to huge new audiences at virtually no cost.

At the same time, celebrity endorsements and involvement gave pickleball an aura of trendiness. When famous figures not only talk about a sport but actively invest in it, people take notice. Over the last few years, a who's-who of athletes and entertainers have publicly aligned themselves with pickleball. NBA legend LeBron James, NFL great Tom Brady, and tennis icon Kim Clijsters all bought ownership stakes in Major League Pickleball (MLP) teams in late 2022. They were soon joined by the likes of Super Bowl champion Drew Brees, NBA stars Draymond Green and Kevin Durant, and even Hollywood actors Eva Longoria, Michael B. Jordan, and Grammy-winning artist Drake – all of whom have invested in professional pickleball franchises or leagues. These big names not only bring money but also bring *spotlight*. Sports media and talk shows began covering pickleball's celebrity backers, further amplifying the sport's profile. It suddenly wasn't uncommon to hear a late-night comedian joke, "Everyone from Patrick Mahomes to your local librarian is playing pickleball these days." The celebrity cachet helped pickleball shed any remaining image of being just a quaint retirement hobby; instead, it became *the hot new thing* that even superstar athletes were betting on.

Hand-in-hand with celebrity interest came the formation of professional leagues and tournaments – a crucial component of pickleball's recent growth spurt. While casual play drives the base, having a professional tier brings legitimacy, media coverage, and aspiration for fans. In 2019, the first pro tour (the PPA – Professional Pickleball Association) launched, and by 2021 Major League Pickleball was founded as a team-based competition. The fact that these happened just before and during the boom is no coincidence: they gave structure to the sport's elite side right as masses of new players were looking for heroes to follow and events to watch. The past few years have seen prize money at tournaments soar, livestreams and even network TV coverage of pickleball matches, and a unification of the pro circuit under robust investment. In 2023, the two major U.S. pro tours (MLP and PPA) announced a merger backed by $50 million in new funding from investors spanning sports and tech. The merged entity boasted team owners across industries – including billionaire tech entrepreneurs and sports team owners – and aimed to streamline a full season of events. *"Tournaments and leagues continue to expand, attracting high-profile investors, sponsors, and former pro athletes from other sports,"* observed one report, noting that with *"more prize money, TV coverage, and corporate backing, pickleball is evolving into a legitimate professional sport with a dedicated fan base."* This rapid professionalization fed back into the boom: casual players, especially the competitive-minded, got even more excited seeing that pickleball had "made it" to the big leagues. Courts are now filled not just with folks out for fun, but also with fans wearing pickleball pro jerseys and quoting the latest rankings of the top players. In short, a virtuous cycle formed – the more people played, the more the sport grew in visibility and organization; the more visible and organized it became, the more people wanted to play.

To summarize, pickleball's moment is *now* because several once-in-a-generation trends aligned. A global pandemic drove people to the sport for safe recreation and stress relief. Social shifts made a casual, social sport more appealing than rigid traditional pastimes. Viral content and celebrity enthusiasm gave pickleball an unprecedented platform. And opportunistic building of professional infrastructure made the sport more serious and newsworthy. The result: what might have taken 20 years of slow growth happened in just 2 or 3 turbocharged years. Of course, none of this would have mattered if pickleball weren't inherently enjoyable – but as we've seen, it is precisely the game's fun, inclusive nature that allowed it to capitalize on this moment. The wave has crested, and pickleball now sits firmly in the American zeitgeist.

1.4 From Rec Centers to Boardrooms: Executive Embrace

One of the most striking developments in pickleball's recent rise is how it has transcended the typical sports venues and permeated the corporate world. It's not just retirees playing casual games at the rec center anymore – it's CEOs, entrepreneurs, lawyers, and financiers trading their business suits for moisture-wicking polos and hitting the courts. In some circles, pickleball has even been dubbed "the new golf" as the go-to sport for networking and deal-making. This section explores how and why busy professionals and companies are embracing pickleball, and how the sport has become as much a fixture in boardrooms and company retreats as it is in public parks.

Visit any upscale suburb or city tech hub, and you might find that the tennis courts are being joined (or replaced) by pickleball courts, sometimes even on corporate campuses. For example, in northern Virginia, an office park near Washington D.C. recently filed plans to add two pickleball courts *on a rooftop terrace of a parking garage*, exclusively for use by its office tenants. Providing pickleball facilities is seen as a perk to attract companies and their employees – a modern amenity like a gym or cafe. Major employers have taken note of pickleball's popularity and the social wellness benefits it offers workers. Some companies now sponsor intra-office pickleball leagues or reserve local courts for team outings. From Silicon Valley to Wall Street, the sport is becoming a trendy way to mix business with pleasure.

Why are executives so drawn to pickleball? In part, it's because pickleball fits perfectly into a professional's busy schedule and networking needs. Unlike golf – the classic business sport that can consume half a day – a pickleball match can be played in under an hour, and you don't need to travel to a country club to do it. Companies have realized they can host a fun tournament in a morning and everyone is back to work after lunch, making it a time-efficient bonding activity. *"Pickleball games are shorter than golf, so if you don't have a full day to spare, you can meet over pickleball for as little as an hour... Efficient and productive!"* one club manager noted, emphasizing the sport's appeal to time-crunched professionals. The game's brisk pace and casual setting foster more interaction in less time. Executives report that in an hour of pickleball doubles, they laugh, high-five, and converse more with their partner and opponents than they might over several hours of a formal golf outing. This makes the networking *quality* high even as the time commitment stays low.

Pickleball is also wonderfully inclusive and unintimidating, which matters greatly in a business networking context. Traditional golf outings, while enjoyable for some, can feel exclusive or daunting to others – not everyone grew up learning golf or has access to a course. In contrast, pickleball welcomes beginners with open arms. As Bloomberg reported in a piece aptly titled "Companies Are Ditching Golf for Pickleball," corporate bookings at pickleball clubs have surged precisely because the sport is easy for newcomers and far more inclusive. *Lawyers, bankers, and realtors* are all using pickleball to expand their professional networks. One real estate broker noted that a big advantage of pickleball as a client entertainment activity is that *"pickleball can be enjoyed by beginners within minutes, unlike golf, which can be intimidating for novices".* You can invite a mix of people – perhaps a few seasoned player colleagues and some first-timer clients – and everyone can participate without feeling left out or embarrassed. The smaller court and doubles format mean a weaker player isn't isolated; they have a partner and close proximity to others, making it feel like a group game rather than a solitary struggle. This dynamic helps *break down hierarchies and barriers* that might exist in a formal office setting.

A junior associate can comfortably team up with a senior VP on the pickleball court, and the usual titles matter less than the teamwork and friendly competition at hand.

Corporate America has also noticed that pickleball can promote diversity and inclusion in networking. Golf, for all its business utility, has historically skewed male and often excluded those who didn't have the means or exposure to learn the game. Pickleball, by contrast, is drawing a much more diverse crowd. In many cities, the after-work pickleball scene includes roughly equal men and women, and players from a wide range of ethnic and professional backgrounds. Bloomberg's report highlighted that golf's demographic remains predominantly white and male, *"prompting some executives to turn to pickleball to reach a more diverse group of clients."* The report noted that pickleball offers a *"less formal, more engaging environment, fostering camaraderie and breaking down barriers among participants."* In essence, it's a more modern networking tool that aligns with today's emphasis on inclusive relationship-building. A life coach who works with female executives shared that pickleball has been a refreshing alternative to golf for her clients – it's more accessible and helps women, in particular, expand their professional circles in a traditionally male-dominated networking arena.

Companies themselves are actively encouraging the pickleball trend. Beyond just renting courts, some firms are building courts on-site. Tech giants known for lavish campuses have painted pickleball lines in their sports facilities, and forward-thinking office park developers are including pickleball in their amenities. In one striking example, the recently opened Pickleball Club of Tysons (an indoor club in the Washington D.C. metro area) reported that in just the first few months of operation it hosted *"dozens of corporate neighbors for team-building and social events on our courts. This is the perfect way to engage both clients and employees,"* the club noted of the enthusiastic response. Instead of a happy hour, companies are opting for a pickleball social – employees get exercise, learn a new skill together, and mingle in a low-pressure setting. Human resources departments have taken note of pickleball as a tool for wellness and morale; some offer free clinics or equipment for staff. It's not uncommon now to hear of law firms running intra-firm pickleball ladders (friendly competitive rankings) or startups holding "pickleball Fridays" to unwind at week's end.

High-profile business leaders have themselves become pickleball evangelists. John Mackey, the founder of Whole Foods Market, has spoken about being *"obsessed"* with pickleball in his retirement and even likened it to the new golf in terms of networking and personal challenge. He and other CEOs participate in invite-only pickleball meetups where deals might be discussed between serves. Recognizing this, an enterprising group of entrepreneurs created the Founders League – an exclusive national pickleball league specifically for startup founders and CEOs to compete and connect. In just a couple of years, Founders League exploded to 1,000+ members across 10+ cities, representing companies with a combined enterprise value over $100 billion. The league organizes seasonal matches where founders pair up with partners (often colleagues or fellow execs) and play weekly games, culminating in championship tournaments. The appeal is obvious: where else can a

CEO of a tech company casually mingle and bond with dozens of peers outside of stiff conferences or golf outings? On the pickleball court, everyone is in athletic gear, a bit out of their comfort zone, and able to connect as people first and business leaders second. It's competitive, yet lighthearted – perfect for building relationships. As one Founders League organizer put it, *"We're building a community of peers who share a passion for both business and pickleball"*, noting that the league offers *"fun and competitive play"* for all skill levels of executives. The success of Founders League – and similar CEO pickleball clubs popping up in other industries – underscores how deeply the sport has penetrated the upper echelons of the business community.

It's not an exaggeration to say that pickleball has become the new "water cooler" or golf course for networking. *"Meeting at the pickleball court shows your guests you are health-conscious, active, social, and trendy,"* writes Jen Azevedo, a club general manager, noting that many of those picking up paddles are in the peak of their careers. She enumerates reasons why pickleball is supplanting golf for today's professionals: it's *inclusive* (you meet people at all levels of business on the court), *addictive and fun* (so it quickly builds camaraderie), *affordable* (no costly gear or club fees required), *hip and trendy* (playing it signals you're up on the latest craze), *upbeat in culture* (games are filled with laughter and casual banter), *accessible to newbies* (no one needs years of training to be decent), and *great when pressed for time* (short games allow for networking without killing a whole workday). Indeed, pickleball checks many boxes that align with modern corporate culture: wellness, team-building, inclusivity, efficiency, and just plain fun.

A few anecdotes drive the point home. In Silicon Valley, venture capital firms have started hosting pickleball mixers for founders and investors – a far cry from the staid wine-and-cheese networking events of old. One such event saw young startup CEOs rotating partners on the court, in between quick pitches about their companies during water breaks. Relationships (and deals) were forged in a setting that felt more like play than work. In New York, a major investment bank rented a handful of indoor pickleball courts for a recruiting event, inviting MBA students to meet bankers in a pickleball round-robin; the informal competition eased conversations and gave the firm a hip, approachable image to recruits. And in Miami, a law firm partner recounted how inviting a hesitant client to try pickleball helped break the ice on a sensitive negotiation – *"She'd never played before, but by game two she was laughing and we had a rapport. It absolutely improved our trust when we got back to the conference room."* These stories mirror what the data and trends suggest: pickleball has moved from the recreation realm into the professional toolkit.

In later chapters, we will dive deeper into how high-achievers are leveraging pickleball for strategic advantage – from networking hacks to leadership lessons gleaned on the court. But even at this early stage, it's clear that the executive embrace of pickleball is not just hype. Companies and professionals have found genuine value in the sport, whether as a networking platform, a wellness outlet, or a means to build team spirit. Pickleball has effectively *entered the boardroom*, symbolically and sometimes literally (one can imagine pickleball paddles propped in the corner of office suites these days). The same qualities that make the game accessible to all – its brevity, simplicity, and social nature – make it perfect for busy leaders looking to connect with others in a meaningful way.

As we wrap up this chapter on the pickleball phenomenon, consider this: a sport invented in a backyard almost 60 years ago has, in a very short span, become a mainstay of American life from the grassroots to the executive level. The meteoric rise of pickleball is a story of convergence – of a game that meets a cultural moment, of fun intersecting with purpose, of community blending with competition. It's being played in schoolyards and senior centers, on city sidewalks and suburban clubs, by Hollywood stars and hard-working CEOs alike. And underlying all the trends and stats is a simple truth any pickleball player will tell you with a smile: *it's just an incredibly fun game.* That joy is what ultimately propels the phenomenon forward. Busy professionals, retirees, and teenagers are all finding in pickleball a source of motivation, friendship, and inspiration. The paddle has become a great equalizer – a tool that brings people together and breaks down barriers, whether on a public court or a corporate campus. In the chapters to come, we'll explore how this unifying sport can be leveraged for personal and professional growth. But for now, one thing is certain: the pickleball craze has only begun, and everyone – from park enthusiasts to power brokers – is invited to the party.

Chapter 2

The Physical Edge – Building Your Body with Pickleball

A quick pickleball match provides a surprisingly effective full-body workout. Because it's a low-impact sport, it's easier on the joints than high-impact activities. Yet even a 30–60 minute session can reach moderate to vigorous intensity levels, contributing to heart health and significant fitness gains for busy professionals.

For time-crunched professionals, pickleball offers an efficient way to stay fit without sacrificing fun or hours of your day. It may have a quirky name, but don't be fooled – pickleball can truly make you break a sweat. In fact, this paddle sport has earned respect as a serious workout, attracting everyone from top executives to star athletes. Even world-class competitors like Serena Williams and LeBron James have publicly touted their love of pickleball, and high-profile business leaders are trading their golf clubs for paddles. Why the popularity? Simply put, pickleball delivers a full-body workout that's *grounded in exercise science* yet doesn't feel like tedious exercise. This chapter details the array of physical health benefits pickleball provides – from cardiovascular fitness to improved agility – and explains why it's an ideal workout that can be squeezed into a lunch break. Backed by research and real anecdotes, we'll show how pickleball can keep you in peak shape without the monotony of a treadmill or the soreness of high-impact sports.

Imagine stepping off the court after a quick 30-minute game, heart pumping and muscles engaged, but with a smile on your face. That's the norm with pickleball. Busy professionals find that a few games per week leave them feeling energized rather than exhausted. As Whole Foods founder John Mackey (a famously busy executive in his 70s) discovered, pickleball is *"the new golf"* – a fun outlet for fitness and networking rolled into one. And he's far from alone. Take Utah business owner Ed Wertz, age 71: after his gym closed during the pandemic, Ed's wife invited him to try pickleball for exercise. *"We've played two to three times a week ever since,"* he says. Now Ed gets his workouts in by dinking and volleying on the court instead of trudging on a treadmill. Stories like these prove that pickleball isn't just play – it's a legitimate path to physical vitality at any age. In the sections that follow, we break down the benefits by category, showing how a paddle game can improve your cardio, deliver high rewards with low impact, build strength and agility, and do it all in a fraction of the time of traditional workouts.

2.1 Cardio Workout in a Paddle Game

Pickleball might sound playful, but it packs a real cardio punch. The fast-paced rallies and constant engagement will get your heart rate up in no time. In a typical pickleball exchange – dashing to the net for a quick volley or stretching to return a lob – you'll find yourself breathing harder and breaking a sweat. Don't underestimate it: a friendly pickleball match can be as aerobic as a jog in the park. Researchers have confirmed this with hard data. A study of older adult pickleball players at the University of Manitoba found that playing pickleball reliably raises heart rates into the moderate-intensity exercise zone for most adults. In fact, participants' mean heart rates during games met the criteria for moderate-intensity physical activity, and over 70% of players' active time was spent in moderate to even vigorous intensity ranges. In plain terms, your heart and lungs are getting a solid workout every time you step on the court.

Why is this important? Health experts recommend getting at least 150 minutes per week of moderate-intensity exercise to maintain cardiovascular health. The good news is that just a few pickleball sessions can help you hit that target. Play a couple of games three times a week, and you'll rack up those 150+ minutes almost without realizing it. One analysis noted that an older adult playing about 4.5 hours of pickleball in a week (for example, an hour on three different days) would meet standard physical activity recommendations easily. Even if you can't spare that much time, smaller doses make a difference. A single 30–60 minute pickleball session can elevate your heart rate and contribute meaningfully to your weekly exercise goals. Instead of spending hours on an elliptical or treadmill, many professionals are finding that a lunchtime pickleball game gets their heart pumping sufficiently – and it's a lot more engaging mentally.

Beyond just heart rate, pickleball yields real cardiovascular benefits over time. Regular play strengthens the heart muscle and improves circulation, much like more traditional cardio exercises. In one small program, overweight older adults who started playing pickleball three times a week saw measurable improvements in their blood pressure and cholesterol levels after only six weeks. Systolic blood pressure (the top number) dropped by nearly 5 points on average, and harmful LDL cholesterol levels also declined. These changes indicate better heart health – all achieved through a fun sport instead of medication or extra gym sessions.

Calorie burn is another aspect of pickleball's cardio workout. While exact numbers vary by person and intensity, studies show that an hour of doubles pickleball can burn on the order of 400 calories or more, comparable to many aerobic fitness classes. One research team outfitted middle-aged players with sensors and found they burned about 350 calories per match, with heart rates averaging 108 beats per minute – solidly moderate exercise. For perspective, they noted this is 14% higher heart rate and 36% more calories burned than playing a half-hour of brisk walking. In other words, pickleball provides *more bang for your buck* than a typical walk, making it an efficient cardio workout. And if you really want to boost the intensity, try playing singles. Covering the whole court on your own elevates the workload – players in one study took significantly more steps and hit higher exertion levels in singles compared to doubles. Many pickleball enthusiasts mix in singles games or fast-paced drills to get a high-intensity interval training effect, with short bursts of all-out effort during rallies followed by brief rest between points. This interval-like nature of pickleball play (quick rallies and pauses) can mimic the benefits of HIIT, improving cardiovascular fitness in a time-efficient way.

Perhaps the best part of pickleball as cardio is that you're enjoying yourself the whole time. There's a built-in motivation to keep rallying for that next point, which means you often forget you're even exercising. As one fitness writer noted, when fun and fitness take equal stage, people are more likely to stick with it. Sixty-two percent of surveyed picklers said the primary reason they play is because it's *fun*, and that sense of enjoyment keeps them coming back (89% of baby boomers in the survey echoed this). So while you're giggling over a well-placed shot or strategizing with your doubles partner, your heart is quietly reaping the rewards. You'll come off the court slightly winded, pleasantly energized, and one step closer to your fitness goals – all without the drudgery that often accompanies "cardio workouts."

In summary, pickleball provides a quality aerobic workout disguised as a game. A few sessions a week can help manage your weight and boost your cardiovascular health. Your blood pressure, endurance, and overall heart strength stand to improve, just as they would from jogging or cycling. The difference is that pickleball makes cardio *enjoyable and social*, so you're more likely to stick with it. As busy professionals know, consistency is key – and it's a lot easier to be consistent with exercise when it doesn't feel like a chore. Pickleball delivers that perfect blend of sweat and smiles, giving you a heart-healthy workout before you even realize you've been moving.

2.2 Low-Impact, High-Reward Fitness

One of pickleball's greatest strengths is that it's gentle on the body. Unlike running or high-intensity interval training, which can pound your joints and leave you achy, pickleball is a low-impact sport by design. This means you get all those fitness benefits without subjecting your knees, ankles, and back to excessive stress. For anyone who has felt the toll of years of pavement jogging or the wear-and-tear of high-impact sports, this is a *huge advantage*. With pickleball, you can stay active and fit without the nagging pain or high injury risk that often come with more jarring exercises.

What makes pickleball low-impact? First, the court is smaller and the game involves less running than sports like tennis or basketball. A pickleball court is roughly a third the size of a tennis court, so players simply don't need to sprint long distances for each shot. You'll take plenty of quick steps and lunges, but you won't be dashing baseline-to-baseline constantly. The compact court means even if you've "slowed a step or two," you can cover the ground without overexerting your joints. The rules of the game also limit high-impact motions. Serves are done underhand, not overhead – a gentler motion for the shoulder compared to the explosive overhead serves in tennis. This underhand serve, combined with a lightweight paddle and a plastic ball, reduces the strain on your arm and shoulder. You're not swinging as hard or absorbing as much ball impact as you would with a heavy tennis racquet and pressurized ball, for example. Moreover, there's no aggressive jumping to smash the ball as in volleyball or constant pounding on hardwood as in aerobics classes. The lightweight wiffle-style ball moves a bit slower and doesn't require full-force swings to control, further easing the stress on elbows and shoulders. All these factors make pickleball much easier on the joints than high-impact activities like running, basketball, or high-intensity training circuits.

Medical experts have taken note of pickleball's joint-friendly nature. *"Pickleball is easier on joints compared to other sports,"* says Dr. Lisa Cannada, an orthopedic surgeon, who points out that the smaller court means less ground to cover and the underhand serving motion is far kinder to the shoulder. For older adults or those with knee or back concerns, this matters greatly – pickleball provides a way to exercise vigorously without aggravating old injuries or causing new ones. You can play frequently and regularly, which is key to improving fitness, because there's less fear that today's game will leave you too sore to move tomorrow. Busy executives can pick up games multiple times a week without worrying about the kind of chronic knee pain that a daily running habit might trigger.

Low impact *does not* mean low reward. Despite being gentle, pickleball still offers a full-body workout and significant calorie burn – just delivered in a joint-friendly package. In fact, it checks the box as weight-bearing exercise (you're on your feet moving around), which helps maintain bone density, a critical benefit as we age. Every step, squat, and lunge on the court gives your bones a healthy stimulus without the harsh impact of, say, jumping or sprinting on concrete. Dr. Cannada notes that because pickleball is weight-bearing but not too jarring, it can help players maintain bone strength while avoiding the orthopedic injuries that sometimes come with higher-impact sports. This makes pickleball particularly appealing for middle-aged and older professionals who want to stay fit and strong but also stay injury-free.

Let's talk calories and muscles: playing pickleball can burn hundreds of calories and engage muscles across your body, *all with less strain* than comparable activities. A 150-pound person might burn roughly 250–350 calories in a brisk 30-minute pickleball game – similar to the burn rate of jogging, but with far less pounding on the joints. The sport's design naturally spreads the effort to different muscle groups (legs, core, arms) so no single area is overtaxed. Consider a typical rally: you shuffle sideways or jog a few steps (working your legs), rotate your torso to swing (engaging your core), and strike the ball with your arm (working shoulders, forearm, and upper back muscles). It's a compound movement that recruits multiple muscles at once, yet none of those movements are extreme or highly repetitive in a way that would cause stress injuries. Many pickleball players find they can play for hours a week and *feel tired* in a good way – from exercise – but not battered. There's a satisfying "worked out" feeling, without the sharp joint pain or excessive soreness that might follow, say, a game of full-court basketball or an intense plyometrics class.

Another plus: lower risk of overuse injuries. Running daily on pavement can lead to shin splints, tennis can inflame your elbow, and HIIT bootcamps can tweak your knees – but pickleball's moderate pace and low-impact nature reduce these risks. Of course, like any sport, injuries can happen (a misstep or an awkward reach could still cause a strain). However, most pickleball-related injuries tend to be minor and manageable with rest. There's a reason health publications sometimes caution older new players to warm up and avoid backpedaling – it's usually *preventable slips or muscle pulls* from inexperience that cause issues, not the sport itself. By and large, pickleball lets you reap the fitness rewards without the wear-and-tear. As Dr. Edward Laskowski of Mayo

Clinic puts it, as long as you move comfortably and don't have significant balance or pain issues, *"you likely will enjoy pickleball safely"*. It's a workout you can look forward to, not dread. For busy people who can't afford downtime from injury, this low-impact aspect is pure gold – you get your exercise in, stay limber and strong, and come back the next day for more, all while protecting your joints for the long run.

In essence, pickleball is high-reward fitness with minimal strain. It proves you don't have to punish your body to improve your body. Each session elevates your heart rate, works your muscles, and burns calories – but it *feels* playful and sustainable. You can push yourself to sweat knowing that the soft court surface, the slower ball, and the nature of the game are all buffering you from the hard jolts and impacts that other sports impose. For anyone seeking longevity in their fitness routine (and with careers to manage, who isn't?), pickleball is a smart choice. It's a workout that leaves you invigorated, not incapacitated. As one tagline goes, pickleball might just be "the most fun way to age well", keeping you fit and pain-free at the same time.

2.3 Strength, Agility, and Balance

Beyond cardio benefits, pickleball also hones your strength, agility, and balance – often without you even realizing it. Every time you play, you're engaging a wide range of muscles and skills. Think of pickleball as a form of functional fitness: it builds the kind of strength and coordination that directly translate to better mobility and posture in daily life. Instead of isolated gym exercises, you're training your body through dynamic movements – starting, stopping, lunging, twisting, and reacting.

Over time, this pays off in stronger muscles, quicker reflexes, and improved balance that helps you in everyday activities (from climbing stairs to carrying groceries) just as much as it helps you win points on the court.

Let's start with strength. While pickleball isn't a brute-force sport, it does work both your lower and upper body in subtle but effective ways. *"Pickleball is a great workout for the whole body as it works both lower and upper extremities,"* notes Emily Hemendinger, a sports medicine expert. Consider the lower body: each game involves plenty of squats and lunges – whether you're crouching low to return a dink or taking a quick lunge step to reach a shot. These motions engage your quadriceps, hamstrings, and glutes (thighs and buttocks), building leg strength and power. You'll also do a lot of side-to-side shuffling and forward-backward footwork, which works the calves and stabilizing muscles in your hips and ankles. Over time, players notice their legs getting stronger and more toned from all those micro-sprints and directional changes. Now the upper body: swinging the paddle engages muscles in your shoulders (deltoids), chest (pectorals), and arms (biceps/triceps). While the paddle is light, the repeated volleys and smashes provide enough resistance to build muscular endurance in the arms and shoulders. Even your upper back (scapular muscles) gets involved when you reach up for a lob or stretch wide for a shot. Crucially, your core muscles tie everything together – every twist of your torso to hit the ball works your abdominals and lower back. In fact, pickleball players are constantly rotating their core to drive shots or to quickly change direction. This means a stronger midsection that supports your spine. As one trainer put it, *every time you run, jump, or move in different directions on the court, multiple muscle groups fire, promoting positive adaptations throughout your body.* Over weeks and months of play, you'll likely find you've built lean muscle and improved muscle tone, without ever lifting a dumbbell in a gym. It's no wonder regular players report feeling physically stronger and more capable – pickleball sneaks in strength training under the guise of a game.

Now on to agility and reflexes. Pickleball's quick, stop-and-go nature is a perfect recipe for developing agility. During a single rally, you might sprint forward toward the net, then suddenly have to shuffle back, or cut to the left or right to chase a tricky angle. These rapid changes in direction improve your footwork and coordination. At first, you may feel a half-step behind on fast exchanges, but keep at it – your body adapts. Over time, you'll notice you can change direction more fluidly and react to the ball faster. Your feet learn to stay in a "ready position" (knees bent, weight on the balls of your feet), which is a hallmark of agility training. In essence, pickleball trains you to be light on your feet. The short court also means you need quick reflexes, especially when volleying at the net. Balls can zip back and forth in a blink, and your hand-eye coordination steps up to the challenge. You'll get better at tracking the ball and responding almost instantaneously with your paddle – skills that translate to quicker reaction times off the court as well. Many executives who play comment on how their newfound agility helps them stay sharp and alert in other aspects of life too (even if it's just quick footwork to catch an elevator!). As Dr. Laskowski from Mayo Clinic emphasizes, pickleball provides movement that improves hand-eye coordination and agility. It's a fun way to sharpen those skills we often neglect in adulthood.

Perhaps the most profound gains are in balance and stability. Pickleball requires you to move in *all directions* – forward, backward, sideways – and often to do so quickly while maintaining control. This multidirectional movement is fantastic for training your balance. Each time you lunge for a low ball or stretch high for a smash, you're challenging your body's stability. The sport also forces you to continually adjust your foot positioning and stay aware of your center of gravity (especially when maneuvering near the non-volley zone line, aka the "kitchen"). According to experts, all these aspects of pickleball contribute to better balance and proprioception (your sense of body position). One physician noted that playing the game regularly strengthens the vestibular system – the inner-ear balance mechanism – which is *critical to preventing falls* as we get older. In simpler terms, pickleball teaches your body how to stay upright and stable during dynamic movements. You may find that after a few months of playing, you're more sure-footed on uneven ground or less likely to trip over obstacles in daily life. Senior business leaders who have taken up pickleball often remark how their balance has improved – they feel steadier when standing from a chair, or more confident walking on an icy sidewalk in winter. That's functional fitness at work. The improvements in balance aren't just anecdotal; studies on older pickleball players back it up: regular play led to better postural stability and even improved one-leg balance tests.

Pickleball also integrates these elements – strength, agility, balance – all at once, which is why it's so effective. *"It's all integrated,"* as one sports medicine doctor described, *"pickleball is fantastic for getting that entire system coordinated and refined".* You're not just training muscles in isolation; you're training your nervous system to coordinate multiple muscle groups while maintaining stability. This is exactly the kind of training that helps you in real-world scenarios, whether it's quickly stepping around a puddle or maintaining your balance while reaching for something on a high shelf. In essence, pickleball is teaching your body to move *better*.

For example, imagine a fast volley exchange at the net: your leg muscles fire to position you, your core stabilizes your torso, your eyes track the ball, and your arm reflexively reacts to return the shot. All of that happens in a second or two. It's a high-level coordination challenge, and doing it regularly makes your body much more capable. As a result, even players in their 60s or 70s often find themselves with improved reflexes and confidence in their movements. They might notice, *"Hey, I can turn quickly to grab a falling object now without stumbling,"* or *"I feel more secure on my feet in a crowded train."* These are the subtle life enhancements that come from better agility and balance thanks to pickleball.

If all this sounds a bit like athletic training – it is! Pickleball essentially gives you a sports conditioning session disguised as recreation. It builds leg and core strength akin to doing lunges and planks, improves agility like a ladder drill might, and enhances balance similar to a yoga class – but all at once and with the excitement of competition to keep you going. And remember, you don't have to be a superstar athlete to reap these benefits. People of *all fitness levels* improve gradually by playing. We've heard of a 65-year-old finance VP who initially struggled with agility on court; after months of play, he proudly noted he could now *"hop off a curb without feeling wobbly."* Another executive in her 50s reported that the arm strength and stability she gained from pickleball made carrying her laptop bag and stacks of documents feel easier – a small quality of life improvement she hadn't anticipated. The short bursts of action on the court really do add up to stronger muscles and better coordination.

To sum up, pickleball makes you stronger, quicker, and more balanced, all through the medium of play. It's stealth fitness: you build strong legs, a stable core, and nimble feet while having a blast. The sport's stop-go nature develops *power* in your lower body and *precision* in your upper body. The lateral movements and mindful footwork dramatically improve your *balance* and *agility*. These gains not only help you win points and prevent injury on the court, but they translate to a more capable you in daily life. As your muscles tone up and your reflexes sharpen, don't be surprised if you carry yourself a little taller and move with a bit more confidence. Pickleball is giving you a physical edge that extends well beyond the game – and perhaps that's its sneakiest benefit of all.

2.4 Fitness in a Fraction of the Time

If there's one thing busy professionals value above all, it's time. We all have only 24 hours in a day, and carving out a chunk of that for exercise can be challenging amid meetings, emails, and family commitments. That's where pickleball truly shines: it delivers fitness in a fraction of the time of many traditional workouts. You don't need an entire afternoon or even a full hour to get meaningful exercise – pickleball can give you a great workout in the span of a lunch break. For the time-crunched, it's hard to beat the efficiency of this sport.

Consider the typical length of a pickleball game. Unlike a round of golf that can consume half a day, or a gym session that might demand an hour or more, a pickleball match is refreshingly short. Most games to 11 points last only about 15–25 minutes on average. In recreational play, you might even knock out a quick game in as little as 10 minutes if rallies are fast. What this means is that you can squeeze in multiple games in under an hour. Play a best-of-three series with a friend, and you'll likely be done in 45 minutes – with plenty of running, swinging, and sweating accomplished in that brief time. This makes pickleball *perfect* for a busy schedule. Got a free half-hour? That's enough time for a spirited game that gets your heart rate up and your muscles engaged. Many professionals are now using pickleball as their go-to lunch break workout – 20 minutes on the court, a quick cool-down, and they're back to the office recharged and knowing they've met their exercise quota for the day.

Let's compare that to other activities. A typical gym workout (including changing, warming up, equipment use, cooling down) often eats up 60–90 minutes. A run might require 30–45 minutes to feel like you've done enough. Even a brisk walk might need an hour to cover substantial distance. Pickleball compresses a lot of activity into a short time window. In one hour of doubles play, players can accumulate thousands of steps and sustain moderate exertion nearly the whole time. On days when pickleball players hit the court, they ended up taking an extra ~3,000 steps on average, according to one study – all those steps packed into the play session. And players spent roughly 86 minutes in an elevated heart rate zone on game days (many obviously play more than one game in a day), almost half of that in their cardio zone (70–85% of max heart rate). These numbers illustrate how efficient pickleball is at keeping you moving. Essentially, rather than slow, steady exercise, pickleball condenses activity into bursts of action that cumulatively add up to a serious workout. It's a bit like interval training: a fast-paced rally followed by a short break between points, then another burst of activity. Your heart rate stays elevated and your body keeps burning calories throughout a session of quick games.

Because matches are short, you can also control the duration of your workout easily. If you only have 20 minutes free, you can play one game vigorously – you'll definitely get your heart pumping. If you have an hour, you can play a round-robin of games with colleagues, which will involve playing and resting in turns, effectively giving you a full hour of moderate exercise. There's an inherent flexibility: you're not locked into a fixed class schedule or a long game that you can't pause. Many pickleballers will tell you: *just a couple of games can leave you pleasantly spent.* And if you need more, it's easy to start another. This modular nature (game = ~15 minutes) is incredibly convenient for fitting fitness into busy days.

Now, consider the efficiency vs. other sports. Golf, long the favored sport of executives, is wonderfully social but notoriously time-consuming – 18 holes can run 4 hours or more, with relatively low physical exertion (mostly walking). In contrast, an hour of pickleball could have you actively moving and swinging for a large portion of that time, burning calories and working your body, and then you're done. Even traditional tennis often takes longer to get a good workout, since points can be shorter and there's more downtime chasing balls on a big court. With pickleball's smaller court and doubles format, there's actually *more continuous action* in many cases, meaning less idle time, more active time. Corporate wellness groups have started to notice this, which is why some companies are installing pickleball courts at their offices or encouraging lunchtime play – employees can get in vigorous activity and be back at their desks within an hour, something not feasible with many other sports. Bloomberg News recently reported that corporate bookings at pickleball clubs are surging because the sport is *"cheaper, less time-consuming – and easier to play"* than golf for networking and team outings. Deals are literally being made on the pickleball court now, because it's a setting where you can break a sweat, have a conversation, and still return to work in a timely manner.

Another way pickleball maximizes fitness in minimal time is through high-intensity bursts. If you're looking for a quick, intense workout, you can treat pickleball like circuit training. For instance, you might play a series of very fast rallies or drills for 10 minutes straight, take a short rest, and repeat. Some advanced players do this to train – essentially using pickleball for high-intensity interval training (HIIT). But even in normal play, there will be rallies that spike your heart rate into higher zones. Remember that variability we mentioned: one study found some individuals hit heart rate peaks that qualify as vigorous intensity during play. So within a half-hour game, you might actually be oscillating between moderate and vigorous exertion, which is great for cardiovascular conditioning. You could get the equivalent of a structured interval workout organically through competitive play. The result: calories are torched, endurance is built, and time flies by.

To give a concrete example of pickleball's time efficiency, picture this scenario: Two colleagues have 45 minutes free between meetings. They head to a nearby pickleball court, spend 5 minutes warming up, then play doubles for 30 minutes, managing to complete two games to 11. In that half-hour of play, each of them has racked up over 2,500 steps, kept their heart rate in the fat-burning zone nearly the whole time, and engaged all major muscle groups. They cool down for 5 minutes, grab a quick drink, and return to work feeling accomplished. They've effectively met their exercise for the day in the same amount of time many people take just to drive to the gym and change clothes. This efficiency is the secret sauce that draws busy people to pickleball – it *fits* into modern life.

Finally, let's not forget the fun factor: because pickleball is enjoyable and social, you're likely to put in more effort and get more out of the time you spend. In a dull workout, 30 minutes can feel endless and you might slog at half-speed. In a fun pickleball game, 30 minutes feels too short and you might play with high intensity without even realizing it. The competitive spirit and camaraderie naturally encourage you to move a lot in a short period. It's common to come off the court thinking, "Wow, we only played for 20 minutes, but I'm breathing hard and my shirt is sweaty!" That's a sign of an efficient workout.

In summary, pickleball offers maximum fitness return on minimal time investment. Its short game format, continuous action, and adaptability to high-intensity bursts make it an ideal exercise for those with busy schedules. You no longer need to block off an entire evening or sacrifice your weekend to stay in shape. A few quick games sprinkled through your week can deliver the cardiovascular, strength, and agility benefits that keep you in peak condition. So next time you think "I don't have time to work out," remember that a paddle, a ball, and 20-30 minutes are all you need to get moving. You don't need half a day on the golf course or a marathon gym class – pickleball delivers health results in an efficient, fun dose. It's fitness on your terms and on your time. And for the modern professional, that is the ultimate edge.

Chapter 3

Game Therapy – Pickleball for Stress Relief and Mental Well-Being

Modern executives often live in a pressure cooker of deadlines, high-stakes decisions, and nonstop digital chatter. The result? Sky-high stress and mental fatigue. Burnout has become a badge of honor in some corporate circles, but it comes at a cost. In this chapter, we explore an unexpected but perfect release valve for all that tension: pickleball. This rapidly growing paddle sport isn't just a fun game – it's frequently described as *therapeutic* for the mind. From the mood-boosting rush of exercise to the simple joy of play and the warmth of social connection, pickleball offers a grounded, effective antidote to executive stress. Scientific studies and personal anecdotes alike attest that a session on the pickleball court can leave you smiling, less stressed, and more mentally resilient by the time you're back at your desk. It's no wonder that many top CEOs are swapping their golf clubs for pickleball paddles; the sport offers everything a busy professional could want – fast-paced fun, easy access, and an unbeatable social element. Let's dive into why "game therapy" through pickleball works so well for stress relief and mental well-being.

3.1: The Stress-Busting Paddle – Endorphins & Escape

Picture this: after a marathon day of meetings and tough calls, you step onto a pickleball court. The sun is setting, and for the next half hour your entire focus boils down to a lightweight paddle, a perforated ball, and the playful challenge of getting that ball over the net. With each serve and volley, you feel the day's worries start to melt away. Exercise is a proven stress reliever, and pickleball is no exception. Physically, your body responds almost immediately – your heart rate climbs into a moderate aerobic zone, triggering a cascade of beneficial biochemistry. Movement cues your brain to pump out endorphins, those famed "feel-good" chemicals that act as natural mood elevators. At the same time, exercise tamps down the stress hormones adrenaline and cortisol that have been flooding your system all day. The result is a near-instantaneous wave of relief and calm. Harvard Medical School notes that regular aerobic exercise *"has a unique capacity to exhilarate and relax, to counter depression and dissipate stress,"* in part by lowering cortisol and sparking endorphin release. In plain terms, a good pickleball rally can literally biochemically scrub stress from your brain.

But the stress-busting power of pickleball isn't only chemical – it's also mental. Many veteran players will tell you that once you start focusing on the ball and your strategy, *work pressures simply evaporate from your mind.* There's only the here-and-now of the game. That intense focus forces you to forget the client emails and quarterly reports waiting on your phone. In this way, pickleball provides an *escape hatch* from rumination. One executive described how the simple act of chasing a wiffle ball around a court transported him to *"a completely different place – one of joy and happiness, free from thoughts of work, stress, or responsibility"*. This kind of immersion is not just anecdote – it's akin to a form of active, moving meditation. For those 30 minutes on the court, you are living fully in the present moment, and the mental relief is palpable. Regular players often report that even a quick game after work clears their head. By the time they return to the office or home, they feel *refreshed and reset*, their perspective clarified and nerves calmed.

Crucially, science backs up these personal experiences. A recent systematic review of pickleball's health effects found significant improvements in players' mental health measures – including reductions in stress and depression and boosts in overall happiness and well-being. In fact, pickleball is showing such promise as a mood-lifting activity that researchers are calling it a "new tool" to improve mental health across different age groups. It's not just small studies, either. One large analysis of data from over 250,000 people (using fitness trackers and surveys) discovered that regular pickleball players had 60% lower odds of reporting feelings of depression compared to non-players – an even greater mood benefit than observed in regular tennis players. These findings reinforce what pickleball enthusiasts already know: a few sets of pickleball function like *productive playtime* for stress relief. The exercise induces a healthy endorphin high and drains away tension, while the mental break from work worries acts like a reset button for your overworked brain. After 30 minutes on the court, you return to your life with a clearer head and lower cortisol, ready to tackle challenges from a calmer state. In essence, the paddle is like a stress-busting wand – swing it a few times, and watch stress diminish both physically and mentally.

3.2: Pickleball as Active Mindfulness – Finding Flow in Play

Have you ever been so absorbed in an activity that the outside world disappears? Time flies, and for those moments you aren't thinking – you're just *doing*. Many pickleball players experience this in the middle of a good game. Psychologists refer to it as the *flow state* – a blissful state of deep focus that highly successful people often chase through meditation or hobbies. The beauty of pickleball is that it can usher you into a flow state naturally, without you even realizing it's happening. When you're dashing to the net for a quick volley or angling your paddle to return a tricky shot, your mind must lock onto the *here and now*. The rapid rallies and the need to react in milliseconds leave no room for dwelling on that budget meeting or tomorrow's presentation. You become fully present, body and mind working in unison. The sound of the ball popping off paddles, the rhythmic back-and-forth of the rally, even the laughter and calls of "nice shot!" between points – all of it anchors you in *the current moment*. In those minutes, worrying about emails or life's problems takes a back seat.

This is why we call pickleball a form of "active mindfulness." Unlike sitting meditation, here the mindfulness is built into the activity. You're effectively practicing mindfulness meditation on the move: focusing on your breath is replaced by focusing on tracking the ball; returning to the present moment happens naturally every time the ball is served. Many busy professionals find this *focus through play* incredibly therapeutic. It's hard to stew over a conflict with a client when you're concentrating on whether to dink or smash a shot across the net. In fact, neuroscientists have found that during a flow state the brain undergoes *"transient hypofrontality"* – essentially, the overactive worrying part of your brain powers down for a while. That inner critic voice in your head goes silent, and your mental energy is fully engaged in the task at hand. It's the same phenomenon experienced by artists, musicians, or athletes "in the zone." All those stress-related thoughts get tuned out. The result is not only improved performance, but a profound sense of *mental quiet and clarity*. Afterwards, players often feel as though they've given their brain a refreshing rest, despite having been highly active.

Pickleball's ability to induce flow is one of its secret gifts to mental well-being. Even novice players can taste this zone when a rally gets exciting. One moment you're thinking of ten things at once; the next, *there is only the ball*. A corporate lawyer who took up pickleball marveled that the game put him in a meditative headspace: *"the simplicity of the game brought my mind to a completely different place – one of joy and happiness, free from thoughts of work…"*. Without sitting on a cushion or chanting "om," he achieved the same *mind-clearing benefits* that mindfulness practitioners strive for. Studies on positive psychology note that achieving flow in leisure activities is strongly associated with reduced anxiety and stress, because it acts as a coping mechanism – your brain gets a break from the chronic stress loop while you engage your skills in something fun. In pickleball, attaining this flow is relatively easy because the game is just challenging enough to demand your full attention, but inherently playful so it never feels like a chore. The quick feedback of each point keeps you engaged and in the present. In many ways, a lively pickleball match *is a form of moving meditation.* You emerge from the court with your mind calmer and sharper – essentially having practiced mindfulness without even trying. For a harried executive, this *active mindfulness* can be a game-changer: it trains your focus to stay in the moment, which carries over into better concentration and calm even after you've left the court.

In summary, pickleball triggers mindfulness through motion. By entering a state of flow during play, you grant your mind a respite from stress and overthinking. This not only leaves you feeling mentally refreshed, but over time can improve your baseline stress resilience and mental clarity. The next time you find your thoughts racing, consider that perhaps the most enjoyable way to practice mindfulness might just be a paddle in hand and a friendly game underway.

3.3: Confidence, Achievement, and Joy – Fueling a Positive Mindset

There's a special kind of joy in learning something new as an adult – especially for high achievers accustomed to long work hours and heavy responsibilities. Pickleball provides that spark of *playful achievement.* It's a low-stakes environment where you can set little goals, see progress week by week, and relish the wins that come your way – all without the pressure of performance reviews or bottom lines. Many executives find that improving at pickleball rekindles their sense of personal achievement and confidence in a way that's fundamentally different from work. On the court, it doesn't matter what your job title is; what matters is that satisfying *thwack* of the ball when you execute a great shot or the laughter that follows a ridiculously fun rally. These small victories on the court can translate into big psychological boosts.

One of the *hidden mental health benefits* of pickleball is how it builds self-confidence and a growth mindset. As you learn the game, you inevitably go from novice mistakes to competent play – perhaps even mastery if you stick with it. This journey sparks the positive feelings that come with skill development. Psychologists note that regular exercise can improve self-esteem partly through such mastery experiences: as your physical skills improve, *"your self-image will improve"* and you gain a sense of mastery, pride, and self-confidence. Pickleball offers this in abundance. For instance, an executive might initially struggle with their backhand, but after a few weeks of casual coaching from friends, they start nailing those backhand shots. That tangible improvement generates a surge of accomplishment. Unlike the high-pressure achievements at work (which often come with stress and expectations attached), achievements in pickleball are pure fun – they belong to you, and they're celebrated in the moment with a fist-bump or a cheer from your playing partners. This can be incredibly refreshing for someone in a high-level job where wins are abstract or far-off. As one player who had been feeling burnt out put it, *"pickleball helped me remember what it's like to enjoy learning again."* The game reintroduces *play* into life, which is something many overworked professionals haven't experienced in years. That playful learning can break the cycle of chronic stress and stagnation that fuels burnout.

Furthermore, the psychological lift from mastering a new skill extends beyond the court. It can change your mindset at work too. High achievers who take up pickleball often report feeling *re-energized* in other areas of life. The confidence gained from seeing improvement in a fun context can restore faith in one's ability to grow and adapt in general. In pickleball, failure is low-consequence (losing a point) and often even humorous, which helps perfectionists loosen up. Over time, this can erode the fear of failure that stress often amplifies. You start approaching challenges – whether a tricky serve or a tough project – with a more positive, can-do attitude. Enjoyment sparks motivation. A 2020 study of pickleball players noted that participants were largely *intrinsically motivated* – they played for the love of the game and the sense of accomplishment it gave them, rather than any external reward. They particularly valued *task mastery* (honing their skills) and reported a strong sense of *achievement* when they improved. This intrinsic joy in progress is a powerful antidote to the extrinsic, pressure-filled world many executives live in.

To illustrate, consider a composite anecdote drawn from many real stories: Jessica, a 45-year-old VP at a tech firm, was nearing burnout after years of nonstop work. At the insistence of a colleague, she joined a weekend pickleball group. At first, Jessica was out of her element – she hadn't played sports in decades. But week by week, she picked up techniques. She remembers the first time she served an ace and the rush of pride it gave her. It was a *pure, childlike joy* she hadn't felt in a long time. Each time she learned a new trick or won a hard-fought point, Jessica's confidence grew. She started to carry herself a bit taller on Monday mornings, and challenges at work felt a little less daunting. Breaking out of her "work-only" mindset and allowing herself to play made her more resilient. Psychologically, she felt *competent* again in a new arena, which reminded her that she could tackle new challenges anywhere. Testimonials like Jessica's are common – people credit pickleball with helping them climb out of a mental rut by *infusing fun and a sense of achievement* back into their lives.

Let's not forget the sheer joy factor as well. Pickleball's culture is famously supportive and lighthearted. A well-placed shot is often met with high-fives and "great shot!" exclamations from teammates and even opponents. This positive reinforcement can counteract the isolation and constant critique that many professionals face in their jobs. Instead of only hearing about mistakes or what needs improvement (a common theme in workplaces), on the pickleball court you're likely to hear praises and friendly encouragement regularly. That *sense of being appreciated* and celebrating little wins with others feeds happiness. Studies on older pickleball players (a group studied often by researchers) have found that the combination of learning a new skill and enjoying the activity correlates with higher happiness and life satisfaction. In other words, *pride in developing a new skill, combined with the pure fun of play, leads to a tangible uplift in well-being.* For executives used to tight schedules and serious stakes, having this joyful outlet can reset their emotional tone. They rediscover laughter, friendly competition, and the thrill of incremental improvement – all of which act as a buffer against stress and a booster for mental health. In summary, pickleball fuels a virtuous cycle: play leads to improvement, improvement builds confidence, and confidence (plus laughter) leads to joy. It's a cycle that can spill over to make you more upbeat and resilient in all aspects of life.

3.4: Social Support and Belonging – A Built-In Community

Perhaps one of the greatest therapeutic aspects of pickleball – and one that busy executives might least expect – is the **social connection** it fosters. It's often said that *"it's lonely at the top."* CEOs and leaders, by virtue of their roles, can become isolated. Workdays leave little time to nurture friendships, and the stress of being in charge can create a sense of disconnection from others. Enter pickleball: a sport that is inherently social and community-oriented. Unlike hitting the gym solo or going on a lone run, pickleball almost always involves other people – typically you play doubles (two per team), and players frequently rotate partners and opponents in casual play. What that means is from the moment you step onto the court, you're part of a *mini support network*. There's banter, teamwork, gentle ribbing, and shared focus with your partner. Between points or matches, people chat, laugh, and get to know each other. Over time, those weekly games turn into real friendships.

Research has shown that this social aspect of pickleball greatly boosts happiness and life satisfaction, especially in older adults who play. In one study of senior pickleball players, the new friendships and social interactions formed on the court significantly enhanced players' overall well-being. The simple act of meeting new people and engaging in a fun activity together reduces feelings of loneliness and builds a sense of belonging. For executives and professionals, these benefits are just as crucial. In fact, the social dimension might be pickleball's *most potent stress-buster.* Human beings are social creatures; having a circle of friends to laugh with, share a high-five, or even commiserate with after a missed shot can dramatically buffer stress. The American Bar Association – an organization not typically known for sports fandom – highlighted that enhancing social relationships through pickleball "contributes to the player's happiness, satisfaction with life, and overall feeling of well-being." This is a powerful endorsement of the sport's community vibe.

What makes the pickleball community particularly special is its inclusivity and camaraderie. Step onto a public pickleball court almost anywhere, and you'll likely be welcomed by the regulars. They'll mix novice players with experienced ones, ensuring everyone gets to play. This isn't a stuffy country club with strict rules – it's more akin to a neighborhood pick-up game where all are invited. For someone in a high-powered job, this can be wonderfully egalitarian. When you play pickleball, your title and resume don't matter; as one article noted, *"once you're on the court, titles don't matter"* – a CEO, an intern, and a retiree are all just players enjoying the game side by side. That break from hierarchical interactions can be refreshing. You get to be *just another person with a paddle,* joking with everyone else. The relief and belonging that comes from this can't be overstated.

Social support is a well-known *protective factor against stress.* Friends and community act as a buffer, providing both emotional support and practical encouragement. Pickleball organically creates those support systems. Consider how a weekly pickleball meet-up can turn into a close-knit group: teammates celebrate each other's improvements, regulars notice if you miss a session ("We missed you last week!"), and groups often end up grabbing coffee or drinks after play. Many pickleball communities extend beyond the court – they organize social events, cheer each other on in local tournaments, and even support members through life's ups and downs. For a busy professional, having this kind of built-in social outlet can be life-changing. It guarantees that at least once or twice a week, you have an *appointment for fun* with people you enjoy – a stark contrast to business meetings.

Studies focusing on pickleball's social impacts have found concrete benefits. Older adults who play regularly report *lower levels of loneliness and higher life satisfaction*, attributing this to the friendships and sense of community the sport provides. In pickleball circles, it's common to hear that players keep coming back not just for the game, but "for the people." That camaraderie delivers stress relief in two ways: laughter and empathy. There's plenty of laughter in pickleball – it's hard to stay stone-faced serious when you're involved in a cheeky kitchen (no-volley zone) exchange or when someone makes an unexpectedly brilliant shot and everyone applauds. Laughter itself is healing; it releases tension and triggers the relaxation response. Meanwhile, the empathy and support from fellow players means that if you've had a bad day, a few kind words or just the company of friends can help put things in perspective. Knowing *"I have friends to play with who care about me"* is a powerful antidote to the isolation stress can bring.

For an executive who might feel they shoulder burdens alone at work, joining a pickleball group can restore a sense of belonging. You're part of a team each time you play doubles, and part of a wider community of enthusiasts. This belonging can greatly enhance mental well-being. When you have a network of friends cheering you on – whether in sport or in life – challenges feel less daunting. In fact, psychologists say high-quality social support enhances resilience to stress and even boosts physical health by buffering the physiological effects of stress. On the court, this dynamic plays out in simple ways: teammates encourage each other ("Shake off that missed shot, you've got the next one!"), and friends notice your mood ("You seem lighter today – did you finally finish that project?"). These small interactions weave a safety net that can catch stress before it spirals.

To tailor this to the executive experience: if you're a leader used to standing alone, a weekly pickleball game can remind you what it's like to have *peers*. In that hour, you're not the boss or the decision-maker – you're a buddy and a teammate. That camaraderie can re-energize you and give a joyful human context outside of work. Many executives find that after forming pickleball friendships, they carry a more positive, connected mindset back into the workplace. The confidence that "I have a life and friends beyond the boardroom" provides emotional stability. And practically speaking, your pickleball pals might become a sounding board or source of encouragement in other areas as well.

In closing, pickleball's social nature might be its most potent mental health benefit. The sport inherently delivers what many stressed professionals are missing: *real human connection and play*. Research confirms that the social bonds from playing significantly boost happiness and reduce feelings of loneliness. In our hectic lives, carving out time for community can fall by the wayside – pickleball makes it fun and easy to reclaim that. The laughter, high-fives, and post-game conversations aren't just enjoyable in the moment; they build a resilient support system around you. Knowing you have friends to play with and laugh with each week becomes a bright spot on the calendar – something to look forward to, no matter how stressful work gets. And that sense of belonging, of being part of a tribe of people who enjoy the same activity, delivers a deep feeling of safety and satisfaction that guards against stress. For the executive "lonely at the top," a pickleball group can feel like finding your people – an *executive therapy group disguised as a sports club*, where everyone leaves happier than when they arrived.

In summary, *Game Therapy* through pickleball works on multiple levels to relieve stress and bolster mental well-being. It gives you the endorphin rush and physical outlet your body craves, the mindful focus that quiets a racing mind, the confidence and joy that come from playful achievement, and the camaraderie and belonging that remind you you're not alone in this hectic world. It's remarkable that a single activity can tick so many mental wellness boxes – but as countless busy professionals are discovering, pickleball truly is therapeutic. After a tough week in the office, the cure might just be a paddle, a ball, and a group of friends saying "See you on the court!" With each game, you're not only having fun and getting fit; you're also training your mind to be happier, more present, and more resilient – a champion of mental well-being both on and off the court.

Chapter 4

Sharpening the Mind – Cognitive Benefits of Pickleball

eyond stress relief, pickleball can actually make you smarter – or at least help keep your brain sharp. Think of each game as a workout for your brain as much as for your body. This chapter explores the cognitive perks of playing pickleball, which range from quicker thinking and better focus to a more resilient memory. The sport combines physical exercise (long known to benefit brain health) with strategic thinking and split-second decision-making. In essence, every time you step on the pickleball court, you're giving your mind a challenge along with your muscles. Busy professionals might discover that regular pickleball sessions enhance their focus, strategic acumen, and even spark greater creativity back at work. It's not just play – it's mental training disguised as fun.

4.1 Strategic Thinking: The Chess Match on Court

Pickleball isn't just about reflexes or physical skill – it's very much a game of strategy. Many enthusiasts describe a good pickleball match as a "chess match at the net," unfolding in real time at the pace of a volley. This means you have to think a few moves ahead, anticipate your opponent's strategy, and decide on the best response – all in a matter of seconds while a plastic ball zips toward you. As a player, you constantly analyze and anticipate: *Where should I place the next shot? Should I hit it softly with a gentle dink or drive it hard past my opponent? Should I aim deep toward the baseline or drop it just over the net?* Each decision has to be made on the fly, and each one can determine whether you win the rally.

Crafting a strategy in pickleball exercises your cognitive muscles in a unique way. Consider what happens in a single extended rally: you might notice that the opposing team's stronger player is lurking on the left side, so you deliberately aim a shot toward the right to force the weaker player into action. You see your opponent moving up, so you decide to lob the ball high over their head to send them scrambling back. Or maybe you've been hitting soft shots (dinks) and decide to suddenly change the pace with a swift, angled drive. In those few moments, your brain is weighing options, predicting outcomes, and executing a plan – very much like a business strategist mapping out a competitive move, but in real time. This kind of rapid-fire strategic thinking under pressure can enhance mental agility. You're effectively teaching your brain to process information and make decisions more quickly.

Research into pickleball notes just how much mental calculation is happening during play. Players have to quickly gauge the speed and angle of an incoming shot, judge whether it's better to volley the ball out of the air or let it bounce, and then decide where to place the return to outwit their opponents' positioning. All of this happens in seconds and repeats every rally. It's like solving a series of tiny puzzles one after another at high speed. Over time, engaging in this "brain game" aspect of pickleball can help keep your mind sharp. You may find yourself thinking one step ahead not only on the court, but also in everyday life.

For busy professionals, the strategic demands of pickleball can have direct carryover to the workplace. The game trains you to think proactively – to anticipate what might happen next and plan for it. That mindset of being one step ahead is invaluable in business strategy and leadership. After regularly playing pickleball, you might notice you're more adept at strategizing during a meeting or coming up with contingency plans on a project. The sport essentially drills the habit of quick strategic assessment: you size up a situation, consider your options, and choose the most effective response. And because all this happens while you're having fun, your brain is learning these skills in a low-stress, engaging environment. It's a form of stealth training for your executive thinking skills. Many players even report that the focus and strategic thinking they practice on the court translates into sharper problem-solving and creative thinking off the court. In other words, that chess match on the court could be training you for the chess match in the boardroom.

4.2 Hand-Eye Coordination and Reflexes

Now let's talk about another side of pickleball's mental workout: the way it fine-tunes your reflexes and hand-eye coordination. Imagine a plastic pickleball hurtling toward you – it might not weigh much, but it can move surprisingly fast, especially in a heated exchange at the net. You have only a split second to react. Your eyes lock onto the ball, your brain calculates its trajectory, and almost automatically your arm moves to position the paddle for the perfect hit. When you pull off a quick volley or a reflex save, you're witnessing the brain and body working in harmony at high speed. This kind of rapid coordination doesn't just happen by luck; it's a skill that grows with practice, and it reflects significant training for your brain.

Fast exchanges on the pickleball court effectively train the connection between your brain and your body. Each time you play, you are honing your hand-eye coordination – the ability of your visual system and your motor control to work together seamlessly. You learn to track the ball's movement with your eyes and instinctively adjust your body and paddle position. Over time, your brain gets better at processing what it sees and sending the right signals to your muscles in a fraction of a second. The result? Quicker reaction times. Many players, even those who start the sport later in life, notice their reflexes becoming sharper. They might find they're more adept at quickly catching a dropped object at home or reacting swiftly to avoid an obstacle while driving. In this way, the reflex and coordination gains from the court carry over to help you stay nimble and alert in everyday life.

There's science to back up these observations. Studies on racket sports like tennis, table tennis, and badminton have found that regularly engaging in these activities can improve neural processing speed and even aspects of vision like tracking moving objects in your peripheral vision. Pickleball, being in the same family of sports, offers similar benefits. It challenges you to respond to a fast-moving target at unpredictable angles, which means your brain is constantly practicing how to filter visual information and act on it almost instantaneously. Essentially, you're training your nervous system to be more efficient. Think of it as calibrating your reflexes – what used to require conscious effort becomes automatic and lightning fast.

For an executive or any professional, sharpening your physical reflexes can also sharpen your mental reflexes. That quick mental turn of speed – the ability to think on your feet during a heated discussion or to come up with a swift solution when a problem arises – can get a boost from sports that train you to react fast. The alertness you cultivate on the pickleball court might mean that in the boardroom or during a tough negotiation, you respond with more confidence and speed. You've conditioned your mind to handle rapid-fire situations without panicking.

Moreover, the concentration needed for pickleball's quick rallies can help improve your focus. You learn to tune out distractions (there's no time to worry about your inbox when a ball is speeding at you) and enter a state of sharp attention. That ability to zero in on what matters can carry over to work when you need to focus amid a flurry of demands.

Another often overlooked benefit is how pickleball can subtly improve your spatial awareness and peripheral vision. As you play, you're not only focusing on the ball but also staying aware of where your partner is, where your opponents are moving, and the boundaries of the court. Your brain is juggling all these spatial details, which can enhance the cognitive skills involved in spatial awareness. It's the same kind of skill that helps a driver sense a car in their blind spot or helps you navigate a crowded room without bumping into people. In pickleball, maintaining this broader awareness while also reacting to immediate challenges is a fantastic exercise for the brain.

4.3 Memory, Learning, and Neuroplasticity

Pickleball isn't just about what you already know – it's about constantly learning and adapting, which gives your brain's memory and learning centers a healthy workout. Think back to when you first learned the game. Even the scoring system in pickleball is a small mental challenge: keeping track of the score and whose turn it is to serve can feel like a brain teaser, especially for beginners. (In pickleball, for example, the server calls out three numbers each time – a quirk that makes scoring a real head-scratcher at first.)

Each time you play, you have to remember the score, follow the rotation of serves, and recall the rules like the double-bounce rule or the non-volley zone ("kitchen") rule. These might seem like small things, but collectively they force your memory to stay active and engaged throughout the game.

Beyond the basics, there's a lot of learning happening every time you step on the court. You might be mastering a new skill, like perfecting a backspin serve or learning to hit a drop shot that just clears the net. You experiment with different strategies – perhaps you discover that a certain opponent struggles with high lobs to their backhand, so you file that info away for future games.

All these little lessons are examples of your brain forming new connections. Neuroscientists call this neuroplasticity – the brain's amazing ability to rewire and adapt by forming new neural pathways. When you challenge yourself with a novel activity like pickleball, especially one that involves both physical coordination and strategic thinking, you're encouraging your brain to strengthen existing connections and to create new ones.

Engaging in a new sport or skill is known to be a great way to promote brain plasticity and keep cognitive function strong. Research on aging and cognition often highlights the importance of "learning something new" as we get older. This could mean learning a language, playing a musical instrument, or yes, picking up a sport like pickleball. The reason is that when you learn new rules, new motions, and new strategies, your brain has to work harder than it does when you're on autopilot with a familiar routine. It's like giving your brain a bit of a puzzle or a problem to solve, which in turn can improve your ability to learn and remember overall. In pickleball, every new tactic you try or technique you practice is a mini lesson for your brain. And because it's fun and engaging, you likely don't even notice how much learning you're doing.

Memory gets a boost from these activities as well. Think about the memory elements involved in playing pickleball. You remember past games – what worked and what didn't. Maybe you recall that last week your colleague (who has a killer backhand) kept beating you at the net, so this week you come prepared to play more shots to their forehand or to hang back a little and hit deeper shots. You might memorize certain plays or patterns, like recognizing "when my opponent is positioned this way, that's my cue to try a soft shot down the sideline." These kinds of recollections and pattern recognitions exercise your memory in a practical, enjoyable way. It's very different from, say, memorizing a spreadsheet of figures for work; it's learning by doing, and it tends to stick better because it's tied to an active experience.

There's also evidence that complex physical activities – those that involve coordination, strategy, and learning – can have positive effects on the brain's structure and function. Aerobic exercise on its own is known to increase blood flow to the brain and stimulate the release of growth factors that help brain cells thrive. Some studies even show that regular aerobic exercise can increase the volume of the hippocampus (the brain's key memory center), essentially giving you more memory capacity to work with.

Now add the layer of skill learning in pickleball, and you're doing double duty for your brain. You're not only keeping the brain cells healthy with exercise, but also forming brand new connections through learning. This combination can lead to better cognitive flexibility – meaning you can switch between tasks or thoughts more easily – and it can improve memory retention because you're continually using your memory in engaging ways.

It's easy as adults to stick to what we're already good at, but learning pickleball is like sending your brain to the gym for a workout. It might be challenging at first – remember how tricky that serve was initially? – but with each game, you can feel yourself improving and picking things up faster. That feeling of progress is your brain adapting in real time. By challenging your mind in different ways than your typical work tasks, you're enhancing overall cognitive flexibility. Many players find that after an engaging pickleball game, they return to work feeling mentally refreshed – as if their brain just had a healthy workout. Whether it's remembering project details, learning a new software skill, or staying sharp in conversation, the habit of adapting on the court helps keep you mentally agile off the court as well.

4.4 Brain Health for the Long Term

The cognitive benefits of pickleball aren't just immediate boosts to focus or memory – they also add up to significant long-term advantages for your brain health. If you play regularly, each session is like depositing a bit of "brain capital" into your future bank of mental acuity. Decades of research in health and neuroscience have shown that consistent moderate exercise is associated with a reduced risk of cognitive decline as we age. In simple terms, people who stay physically active tend to maintain sharper minds and are at lower risk for conditions like dementia and Alzheimer's disease.

Now, pickleball is a great form of moderate exercise – it gets your heart rate up, improves circulation, and makes you break a sweat – so it already checks that box for brain health. But what makes it special is that, as we've discussed, it's not *just* exercise. It's also highly engaging mentally. That means pickleball is hitting a kind of brain health "sweet spot" by combining physical activity with mental stimulation.

Experts often praise activities that merge physical movement with cognitive challenge as ideal for preserving cognitive function. Think of things like dancing (where you have to remember steps) or tai chi (which combines movement with focus) – pickleball fits into that category nicely. You're moving your body, which improves blood flow and oxygen delivery to the brain, and at the same time you're strategizing, coordinating, and socializing. This one-two punch of physical and mental engagement can help build up something researchers call "cognitive reserve." Cognitive reserve is like your brain's resilience or buffer against aging and disease. The more you build it up through enriching activities, the more your brain can handle challenges or potential damage down the line without showing signs of slowing down.

In fact, some early studies specifically on pickleball players are showing promising results for cognitive health. In programs where older adults took up pickleball a few times a week, participants saw improvements in measures of cognitive performance – things like processing speed and executive function – after several weeks or months of play. Processing speed basically means how fast your brain takes in information and responds – being able to think on your feet a little quicker. Executive function covers higher-level skills like planning, multitasking, and problem-solving – the mental toolkit you use to manage complex tasks in work and life.

The fact that a fun sport like pickleball can give a noticeable uptick to these abilities is exciting news. It means that by enjoying yourself on the court, you might also be keeping your brain's toolkit sharp.

Let's put it in perspective: by playing pickleball regularly, you're potentially lowering your risk of serious cognitive decline in the future, while also enhancing your day-to-day mental performance in the present. Aerobic exercise on its own has been shown to reduce the risk of dementia by a substantial margin – some research suggests by roughly 30–40% for those who stay active. When you add the mental layer that pickleball provides, you're essentially doing "extra credit" for your brain. You're not only strengthening your heart and muscles, but also the neural circuits that govern memory, quick thinking, and coordination. Over time, this could translate to a slower rate of brain aging. People often say "use it or lose it" about muscles, and the same goes for the brain: pickleball gives you a fun way to use it, so you're far less likely to lose it.

For high achievers and busy professionals, thinking about the long game is second nature. You plan your careers, your investments, your life goals – why not also plan for a healthy, sharp mind in your later years? Picking up a habit like pickleball can be seen as an investment in your future cognitive health. It's something enjoyable you do now that could pay dividends in mental acuity later on.

Imagine reaching retirement age and still being quick-witted and mentally agile – by playing now, you're laying the groundwork for that future. Even if retirement is far off, it's reassuring to know you're proactively protecting your mind along the way.

In closing, sharpening your mind through pickleball is a win on all fronts. In the short term, you'll likely notice better focus, faster reactions, and maybe even a boost in creativity and problem-solving when you're back at work. In the long term, you're building a stronger, more resilient brain that can serve you well for years to come. All this while having fun, laughing with friends or colleagues on the court, and enjoying a bit of competition. It's a reminder that staying sharp doesn't have to be all serious – it can be as simple as picking up a paddle and playing a game you love. By having fun on the court today, you're investing in a brighter, mentally sharper tomorrow. That's the power of pickleball when it comes to brain health.

Chapter 5

Court Connections – Building Your Network and Relationships

5.1 The New Golf: Pickleball as the Networking Sport

Move over, golf – pickleball is rapidly becoming the go-to sport for networking among today's business leaders. Picture a group of executives and entrepreneurs in athletic gear, laughing and high-fiving on a pickleball court, instead of trudging through 18 holes. Increasingly, leaders are picking up the paddle to forge connections outside the office in this fast-growing sport. Traditionally, golf has been the premier venue for closing deals and wooing clients, but a growing number of professionals find that pickleball saves them time and money *while also being more inclusive and easier to play for newcomers.* From Silicon Valley venture capitalists to local Chamber of Commerce members, pickleball is emerging as the new social hub for professionals to connect and talk business in a fun, relaxed setting.

One of pickleball's biggest draws as a networking tool is its time-efficiency. A round of golf can gobble up five or more hours (plus travel and prep), whereas a pickleball match lasts only about 30–60 minutes. In the time it takes to play one golf outing with the same foursome, you could play several pickleball games with different partners. Many have likened pickleball mixers to the "speed-dating" of networking sports –

quick games and frequent rotations mean you can meet a variety of people in a short span. Businesspeople love that more meetings = more opportunities, and pickleball's brisk pace allows *meeting many people in one afternoon instead of being stuck with the same group all day*. As a Bloomberg report noted, corporate bookings at pickleball clubs have recently spiked as companies realize the sport is cheaper, less time-consuming, and easier for beginners than golf. In fact, one analysis of corporate spending found that pickleball-related expenses grew 155% year-over-year from 2022 to 2023, far outpacing the growth of golf-related spend in the same period. The message is clear: businesses are investing in pickleball as the new networking frontier.

Another advantage is accessibility. You don't need a country club membership or years of practice to enjoy pickleball. The game is easy to learn, with simple rules and a friendly learning curve, so *even a novice can jump in and have fun within minutes*. That welcoming learning curve creates a relaxed, inclusive atmosphere where no one feels left out or embarrassed – a stark contrast to golf, which can intimidate newcomers with its complex etiquette and skill demands. Pickleball courts are also plentiful and often free or low-cost to use, and a decent paddle might cost $20 instead of the hefty investment in golf clubs. This low barrier to entry means anyone from an intern to a CEO can join the game, leveling the playing field socially. "There are several reasons why pickleball is seeing so much success in networking opportunities," observes one work-life reporter. *"It has a low cost of entry, requires less skill, is multi-generational, and is faster to play than… golf."* In short, pickleball's quick, casual format makes it a networking equalizer.

The result is an explosion of corporate pickleball events and leagues aimed at networking. Companies are organizing pickleball mixers, tournaments, and team-building days because they see real benefits. These events are more time-efficient and cost-effective than traditional golf outings, allowing busy professionals to squeeze in networking without blowing the whole day or budget. And unlike a stuffy conference room or formal golf club, a pickleball court's vibe is *informal and energizing*. One Washington Post piece quipped that companies have started holding "pickleball summits" where deals get discussed between serves and smashes. Even Bloomberg has declared, *"Look out golf: Pickleball is coming for your corporate schmoozers."* Executives across various sectors – lawyers, bankers, realtors, tech founders – are using the sport to expand their professional networks. The trend spans from Wall Street to Main Street; for example, the Clarksville, TN Chamber of Commerce hosted a pickleball tournament specifically to encourage local businesses to mingle. *"It's a fun time in a relaxed atmosphere to network and get to know other Chamber members,"* said one Chamber director of their sold-out pickleball event.

Most importantly, the networking pays off. We've heard numerous anecdotes of deals sparked or partnerships formed after a friendly pickleball game. In one instance, a local real estate agent played in a community pickleball event and ended up striking a new collaboration with people who live in her area – all while having a blast on the court. At another networking tournament, an entrepreneur casually mentioned he was looking to form an LLC for a new venture; by pure chance, he found himself playing against a business attorney who offered to help him. *"I just met one playing pickleball. Imagine that,"* he marveled, calling the encounter *"a godsend"*. In the tech world, a startup founder in Brooklyn started a weekly "Tech Pickleball" meet-up with just a few friends. Within weeks it ballooned to over 50 participants each Friday morning, leading to new business for his company, venture capital introductions, and even job opportunities for others in the group. He noted that pickleball is *"the anti-traditional networking event"* – by sharing a fun game, people build authentic connections instead of just exchanging business cards. The takeaway: whether you're courting clients or hunting for a co-founder, pickleball offers a lively, low-pressure setting to build relationships. Professionals from venture capitalists to small business owners are finding that a bit of friendly competition on the court can open doors that a formal boardroom never would. Pickleball is the new golf, and it's quickly becoming the place where business gets done – one quick game at a time.

5.2 Breaking Down Barriers: An Inclusive Social Circle

One of pickleball's greatest strengths as a networking sport is its inherently inclusive vibe. Step onto a pickleball court during open play and you'll see people of all ages, backgrounds, and job titles happily mingling and mixing teams. The sport's simplicity and doubles format naturally throw together players who might never interact otherwise, breaking down hierarchy and social barriers. Unlike formal networking events – where conversations can feel forced and business titles loom large – a pickleball game immediately puts everyone on the same level. It's hard to be intimidating when you're all in athletic attire and on a first-name basis, united by the shared goal of having fun and winning a few points.

Pickleball is notably *less formal and less intimidating* than sports like golf or typical cocktail mixers. The game's culture is rooted in friendliness and approachability. For example, it's not unusual to see a CEO and an entry-level analyst happily team up as doubles partners and exchange high-fives after a good rally. In the office, that kind of camaraderie might never form due to the organizational hierarchy – but on the pickleball court, everyone's just a player. Ego takes a backseat to enthusiasm. A beginner can feel comfortable jumping into a game with more experienced players because the rules are easy to grasp, and the community norm is to be encouraging (there's even a saying in pickleball: "No one cares if you're good, as long as you're fun!"). Indeed, a real estate professional interviewed about corporate pickleball noted that newcomers can *enjoy the game within minutes*, whereas golf can take much longer to learn and tends to intimidate novices. That welcoming environment helps *people who might shy away from traditional networking* come out of their shell on the court.

Another way pickleball expands the social circle is through its diverse player base. Golf has historically been a sport dominated by a narrow demographic (often older, male, and upper-income). Pickleball, by contrast, attracts men and women in roughly equal measure and of all generations. It's common to see teenagers playing with retirees, and grandmothers playing alongside college students. This diversity means when you show up to a pickleball networking event, you're likely to meet people outside your usual professional bubble. As a report summarizing

Bloomberg's findings put it, some executives are turning to pickleball specifically to reach a more diverse group of clients and colleagues, noting that golf's demographic remains predominantly male and white. Pickleball opens the door to connect with women, younger professionals, and people of varied backgrounds in a way golf networking simply hasn't historically. *"The sport appeals equally to men and women, which is different from golf,"* one networking expert pointed out, underscoring pickleball's multi-generational and inclusive appeal.

Crucially, pickleball's casual, lighthearted culture helps dissolve social barriers like job titles or seniority. On the court, it doesn't matter if you're the VP of Sales or fresh out of college – what matters is good sportsmanship and teamwork. Many players find that this relaxed setting encourages more *open communication* and genuine connection than a stuffy office meeting would. The game provides an instant common ground: you can bond over a great volley or laugh off a flubbed serve. That shared experience creates an opening for conversation that feels natural, not forced. *"Networking is the most important thing you can do. But nobody wants to be sold,"* said one marketing professional at a pickleball business mixer. *"Having events like this breaks the ice. It's a lot more fun when you actually have something in common."* On the pickleball court, the common ground *is* the game – and that breaks the ice far better than awkward small talk at a formal networking event.

What's more, the doubles format means you're literally forced to interact and cooperate with others. Every game, you're paired up with a partner (often a random draw in social play), so you quickly learn to communicate and support each other. In one game you might pair with a seasoned manager who gives you a great tip on your swing; in the next, you could be partnering with a summer intern whose energy is infectious. These pairings shuffle often, ensuring you meet a variety of people. Over time, faces become familiar and friendly regardless of their "day job." One player described how joining a local pickleball group led her to meet people she'd never encounter in her usual social circles. For instance, during casual chats between games she discovered one of her fellow players had *just retired from her dream company (Disney) after a 20-year career* – an invaluable contact and mentor she *"never expected"* to find through a sport. Stories like this show how pickleball widens your network beyond the usual suspects. By interacting in an easygoing context, people reveal more of their personalities and interests, not just their job titles, leading to *real connections.* You're no longer defined by your role as "boss" or "newbie" or "client" – you're simply teammates and competitors sharing a fun experience.

Ultimately, pickleball fosters an inclusive social circle where everyone feels they belong. The culture rewards kindness, encouragement, and enthusiasm. This creates a snowball effect: newcomers feel welcomed and keep coming back, bringing their colleagues or friends into the fold. Over time, the pickleball court becomes a melting pot of professions and backgrounds, one where *you might high-five the company CEO on one point and then learn a trick shot from a grad student the next.* Such interactions build empathy and break down preconceived notions. In a divisive world, a sport that gets an analyst and a CEO laughing on the same team is a powerful thing. Many players say they appreciate how pickleball humanizes their colleagues and contacts – *seeing someone's goofy side during a game, or how they graciously handle a loss, tells you more about their character than a formal meeting ever could.* The result is that networks built on the pickleball court tend to be open and genuine, extending beyond the usual clique and enriching everyone involved.

5.3 Teamwork and Leadership on the Court

When professionals step onto the pickleball court for a doubles match, they get more than just exercise – they get a mini-masterclass in teamwork and leadership. The dynamics of partnering up to play can translate into stronger professional relationships and valuable leadership lessons off the court. In this section, we explore how the skills honed in a pickleball doubles game – communication, cooperation, strategy, adaptability – mirror the qualities of effective teams and leaders in the workplace.

First and foremost, playing doubles in pickleball requires constant communication and collaboration. Teammates must talk to each other, call shots, and coordinate their moves at a moment's notice. Think about it: a ball is lofting over the net – you and your partner have a split second to decide who will take it. You might shout "Got it!" or "Yours!" to avoid confusion. Good teams even divvy up responsibilities implicitly (e.g. *"I'll cover the lobs if you guard the net"* becomes understood over time). This interplay demands trust and clear communication. If both players assume the other will get the ball, it will drop untouched – a classic mistake in both sports *and* business teams. As one leadership coach quipped, merely yelling "Yours!" and assuming someone else will handle it is not a winning strategy on the court or in the office. Instead, successful partners learn to proactively take ownership or explicitly delegate tasks – mirroring how great leaders assign roles clearly and ensure everyone knows their responsibilities. A recent corporate team-building guide noted that pickleball forces teammates to *"talk, strategize, and adjust quickly to stay in sync – skills that mirror what's needed for a successful work environment."* In other words, a doubles match is a crash course in working together under pressure, and that experience builds trust and rapport that carry over beyond the game.

Business managers have started to notice these benefits, which is why many are organizing pickleball outings for their teams. A fun game after work can break down silos and improve how colleagues coordinate. One company reported that after months of weekly pickleball meetups, communication among team members became more fluid and supportive back at the office – people were more inclined to huddle and solve problems together, almost like they would on the court. It makes sense: when you've learned to cover each other's weaknesses in a game and celebrate each other's strengths (perhaps one person has a killer smash while the other excels at drop shots), you start instinctively doing the same in workplace projects. Team pickleball builds camaraderie and empathy. In fact, team-building experts have begun recommending pickleball as an ideal activity to boost group dynamics. *Employees who play together communicate better, build trust, and feel more united, leading to better work outcomes and happier teams.* A busy manager might find that inviting their whole department to play in a mini-tournament not only gives everyone a fun break, but also fosters better teamwork when they're back on the job. Colleagues who may have barely known each other across departments suddenly have shared victories and inside jokes ("remember when we rallied 20 shots in that game!"). Those positive bonds pay dividends when it's time to tackle a tough project at work.

Beyond teamwork, pickleball offers rich leadership lessons for those paying attention. Being a good doubles partner is a balancing act between leading and supporting – exactly what good leaders do in professional settings. Sometimes, you need to take charge on the court: for instance, confidently smash an overhead or make the quick strategic decision to shift your positioning. Other times, you shine by lifting up your partner: offering an encouraging "great try!" after a missed shot or setting them up to hit the winning volley. Great leaders behave similarly; they know when to step forward and give direction and when to step back and let their team members take the spotlight. On the pickleball court, players naturally experience both roles. There are rallies where you might cover for your partner's mistake and others where they cover for yours. This fosters a sense of mutual support and accountability. One study on pickleball's impact on leadership development found that the game's doubles format emphasizes cooperation, coordination, and mutual support – essential qualities for successful leadership teams. Participants in the study reported that playing pickleball improved their ability to work with others and *build trust to achieve collective goals*, directly translating those skills to their professional roles. By experiencing teamwork in a fun, low-stakes context, executives can practice and internalize leadership behaviors like *active listening, encouragement, and adaptability* in real time.

To illustrate some key leadership and teamwork lessons from pickleball, consider the following parallels:

- **Communication & Trust:** In pickleball, teams must communicate constantly – calling shots, signaling strategy, or even using non-verbal cues like hand signals. Similarly, in business, clear and open communication is the foundation of trust. A study noted that effective pickleball players excel at communication, which in turn helped them *articulate a clear vision and foster open dialogue* as leaders at work. Every "I got it!" on the court reinforces the trust that your partner will cover their part, just as in the office each team member must trust others to do their jobs.

- **Strategic Thinking & Adaptability:** A pickleball match is fast-paced and ever-changing – teams have to adjust their tactics on the fly. Should you play aggressively or defensively against this opponent? Who should serve first this game? The ability to adapt strategy quickly is a vital leadership skill. The game encourages players to read their opponents and stay flexible, which *"mirrored many leadership scenarios"* requiring quick decision-making under pressure. Leaders learn to anticipate challenges and change course as needed, much like players anticipating an opponent's shot and adjusting position. As one leadership article joked, not every situation needs a 100-mph solution – sometimes patience and a well-placed dink (a soft shot) wins the day. The lesson:

whether on the court or in the boardroom, strategy is a team effort, and adaptability is key.

- **Composure Under Pressure:** Pickleball can get tense – imagine a tie-break at 10-10, everyone's adrenaline pumping. The best players are the ones who stay calm and focused, executing their shots with consistency. This mirrors the composure great leaders show during high-pressure moments at work. Keeping a cool head, managing your nerves, and maintaining a positive attitude even after a mistake are qualities honed in competitive play. A long rally where you're on the defensive teaches resilience: you learn not to panic, to reset and focus on the next shot. One research finding was that overcoming challenges on the court (say, bouncing back from a losing streak) helped players develop resilience and adaptability that empowered them in leadership situations. In both domains, setbacks are inevitable – what matters is recovering with poise and learning from them.

- **"Servant Leadership" & Support:** Interestingly, pickleball's rules offer a metaphor for leadership. In doubles, you can only score points when your team is serving – which subtly rewards the team that takes initiative and "serves" first. Great leaders often adopt a *serve-first mentality* as well, focusing on enabling their team to succeed. Instead of hogging the glory, a wise leader creates opportunities for others to shine – much like a good pickleball partner might set up a perfect shot for their teammate. This servant-leadership approach has been shown to boost team morale and performance. On the court, that might mean feeding your partner an easy ball they can confidently put away; in the office, it could mean providing resources or clearing obstacles so your colleagues can do their best work. Both build a culture of trust and collaboration.

By actively engaging in these roles and scenarios during play, professionals get to practice leadership and teamwork in real time. They might not even realize it, because they're having fun, but the lessons sink in. An executive may discover that in doubles, barking orders at your partner doesn't work as well as positive encouragement – a useful insight for managing people in the office. Or an employee may gain confidence to make a decision under pressure on the court, and later find that same confidence helps in a high-stakes meeting. The court becomes a kind of leadership lab. As one leadership blogger noted, pickleball provides a modern arena to instill old-fashioned values like integrity (making honest line calls) and fairness, as well as modern teamwork habits. A CEO who regularly plays with their staff might demonstrate graceful winning and losing, showing that it's okay to be competitive yet humble – a duality that earns respect in any context.

In summary, a doubles pickleball match encapsulates many elements of effective teamwork and leadership: communication, strategy, trust, adaptability, and shared accountability. Companies that embrace pickleball outings often find that colleagues return to work with stronger bonds and improved collaboration. And for the individual leader, the game offers a chance to both teach and learn. Sometimes you lead the rally, sometimes you support – but in all cases, you're working as a team, which is exactly the mindset great leaders foster in their organizations. So the next time you're on the court, remember: every point won is a testament to partnership, and every friendly "Nice shot!" you give is building the kind of positive team culture that any workplace would be lucky to have.

5.4 Community and Camaraderie

Many people who pick up pickleball expecting just a fun pastime end up discovering something deeper: a community. What begins as a weekly game can blossom into a network of genuine friendships and a support system that extends well beyond the sport itself. In this section, we describe the strong camaraderie that forms among regular pickleball players and how those connections can enrich both personal and professional life.

Walk into any local pickleball club or park, and you'll likely feel the *community vibe* immediately. You'll hear people cheering each other on, offering tips to beginners, and making plans for coffee or lunch after the games. It's common to see a newcomer welcomed with open arms, lent a spare paddle, and taught the basics by more experienced players. Pickleball is a vibrant community builder, fostering a unique blend of camaraderie and inclusion that brings together people of all ages and backgrounds. Often, local pickleball groups start with just a few enthusiasts and quickly grow into thriving collectives. In these groups, beginners and veterans share not just the court but also stories, advice, and laughter. Strangers who meet on the pickleball court frequently leave as friends – a testament to the sport's inclusive and social nature. Unlike some activities where newcomers might feel isolated, pickleball's culture practically insists that everyone join the fun.

One of the reasons pickleball fosters such camaraderie is the sheer amount of interaction it encourages. The courts are small, so everyone is physically closer, which naturally sparks conversation. Between points or waiting for your next match, there's plenty of opportunity to chat. Those sidelines conversations often flow easily – starting with the game ("Wow, great rally! How long have you been playing?") and often veering into personal territory ("...and what do you do for work?" or "...how are your kids doing?"). In a way, playing together breaks down the usual formalities and lets people connect as humans. A club organizer in Orlando observed that their pickleball networking event had *"a little bit of competition, a lot of community,"* with just enough structure to let connections happen organically. Players rotated partners frequently, and those sitting out had a shaded area to mingle, creating a natural rhythm where *"play led to connection, and connection led to possibility."* The atmosphere was more like a friendly neighborhood block party than a formal networking session – and that's exactly what made it effective.

Networks built through pickleball often extend beyond professional needs – they become genuine friendships. Colleagues who start playing weekly might find themselves celebrating each other's personal milestones off the court. It's not unusual for a pickleball group to organize social gatherings: post-game beers, birthday get-togethers, or even family picnics. In these settings, people who met through the sport end up supporting each other in myriad ways. Mentoring relationships form naturally – an experienced businessperson might take a younger player under their wing career-wise after months of chatting and playing together. Likewise, personal support emerges; for instance, when one regular's spouse was ill, other players stepped in to offer help and meals. The key is that pickleball builds bonds based on mutual enjoyment and respect, not just transactional business card exchanges. As one community-focused article put it, the pickleball court is a space where *"laughter, encouragement, and a sense of belonging are as important as the score."* That sense of belonging keeps people coming back and solidifies pickleball's status as more than a game – it's a social lifeline.

We also see that pickleball tends to break down barriers among participants, leading to open conversations that might not happen in a formal office or networking event. The casual setting and shared activity make people more relaxed and authentic. A blog from a pickleball club noted how the sport's less formal, engaging environment *fosters camaraderie and breaks down barriers* – professionals find themselves chatting openly with folks they might never approach in a suit-and-tie setting. One executive shared that after playing regularly for several months, he had met dozens of new contacts from different industries just by rotating partners each game. He joked that he now knows a go-to person for almost anything – a banker, a graphic designer, a school principal, a tech startup founder – all thanks to the eclectic mix at his local pickleball courts. These are connections he might never have made in his insular work circle. Another player from the Orlando event reflected on how people came *"open to meeting someone new in a way that didn't feel forced."* The result was serendipitous encounters like a chance meeting between a player and an attorney who helped him start his business, or a real estate agent finding new collaboration partners, all through organic play. *"It's not about hitting a quota or collecting business cards,"* the event organizer noted. *"It's about creating the right environment and letting people show up as themselves. The relationships that come from that are real and they stick."* In pickleball's community, people show up as their genuine selves – in sneakers and T-shirts, struggling and succeeding together – and that authenticity forms the basis of strong, lasting relationships.

A powerful aspect of the pickleball community is how it becomes a support system. The network you build on the court isn't just for swapping LinkedIn contacts; it often becomes a group of friends who care about each other's well-being. Regular players celebrate each other's victories (both on and off the court). For example, if someone in the group gets a promotion or lands a big client, you might see a round of applause during the water break. Conversely, when someone faces a challenge, the group rallies – one player described how when he was between jobs, his pickleball friends not only offered leads and referrals but also much-needed encouragement to keep his spirits up. In this way, the camaraderie turns into real community. Local pickleball clubs and leagues often reinforce this by creating a sense of belonging. They might have social media groups or group chats where members exchange tips, organize car-pools, or share life updates. It's not uncommon for these networks to evolve into professional opportunities organically – a casual mention that someone's company is hiring can easily lead to a referral for a pickleball buddy, for instance. As one tech founder said, *"Anytime you mention the word pickleball, it forever builds your network with other people who play."* The shared passion acts like a glue, connecting individuals in a way that's both fun and meaningful.

In summary, pickleball offers more than just a workout or a chance to sharpen your dink shot – it opens the door to a broader, more supportive network. It is a network rooted not in obligation or superficial exchanges, but in mutual enjoyment and genuine respect. Players meet as partners or friendly opponents and often end up as friends. They create a community where professional titles matter less than good sportsmanship, and where the simple act of playing together can lead to mentorship, collaboration, and lasting friendship. For many, this has profoundly enriched their personal and professional lives. They find themselves with a circle of contacts they can lean on, learn from, and laugh with – people they might never have known if not for that first leap onto the pickleball court. That is the magic of the pickleball community: it turns a paddle and a plastic ball into a conduit for human connection. And in a world where genuine connection can be hard to come by, that sense of *camaraderie* is as valuable as any business deal ever made on the court.

Chapter 6

From Court to Boardroom – Leveraging Pickleball in Business Strategy

Pickleball isn't just a pastime for weekends or retirement communities – it's swiftly becoming a secret weapon in the professional world. Busy executives and companies are discovering that the same game sparking joy on the court can ignite wellness, teamwork, and even deal-making off the court. In this chapter, we explore how pickleball is being integrated into corporate life and professional development. Through concrete examples and inspiring case studies, we'll see how a simple hobby can transform into a strategic tool for career and company success. The tone here is grounded and informative, but also motivational – showing that a bit of play might be the missing piece in your business strategy.

6.1: Corporate Wellness and Team-Building

Forward-thinking companies are embracing pickleball as a dynamic part of their corporate wellness and team-building programs. In an era where employee well-being and engagement are paramount, pickleball offers a fresh solution. For example, Teachers Insurance and Annuity Association (TIAA) revamped its 92-acre Charlotte, North Carolina campus to feel more like a public park – complete with walking trails, disc golf, bocce ball, and pickleball courts – all with the goal of emphasizing employees' physical and mental wellness. By weaving recreation into the office landscape, TIAA encourages staff to get moving and interact outdoors during the workday. The message is clear: wellness isn't an afterthought; it's built into the workplace design.

Pickleball is an ideal centerpiece for workplace wellness programs for several reasons. First, it's extremely easy to learn – anyone from the summer intern to the CFO can pick up a paddle and start rallying within minutes. Unlike sports that require extensive training or natural athleticism, pickleball's accessibility means no one is left on the sidelines. Second, games are short and flexible. A typical doubles game often finishes in 15–20 minutes, making it feasible to fit matches into lunch breaks or quick after-work sessions. Busy employees can get a burst of exercise and fun without committing half a day (a stark contrast to a four-hour round of golf). As one report noted, the game's shorter duration "allows executives to organize events without taking up the entire day, making it easier to fit into busy schedules". Third, it's inherently social. The doubles format and small court size put players in close contact, sparking conversation and camaraderie. Laughter and high-fives are common, and the competitive aspect is friendly rather than intense. In short, pickleball builds team spirit by getting colleagues to bond over a shared activity rather than just sharing emails.

Real-world corporate initiatives underscore these benefits. Many companies have started hosting casual pickleball tournaments or designated "open play" hours where employees from different departments mix on the court. This mingling breaks down silos – a software engineer might partner with a marketing associate, or a senior manager might play against new hires, all in good fun. The result is a workplace where hierarchies soften and new connections form. One retailer, Room & Board, found that installing an on-site pickleball court was a "stroke of genius" for enticing remote-weary staff back to the office. Built years before the sport's current boom, that indoor court became a magnet when employees were asked to return post-pandemic. It significantly boosted in-person attendance and, with it, engagement and morale. At Room & Board's Minneapolis headquarters, about 50 out of 350 employees now play pickleball on a weekly basis. Staff are allowed to use the court anytime – before, during, or after work – with many preferring morning and afternoon games to energize their day. The company even reported hearing the echoes of laughter down the halls during particularly lively matches – a far cry from the usual office hum. Instead of being seen as a distraction, this levity signaled a happier, healthier workplace. As Room & Board's Chief People Officer Nancy Manley explains, "We don't want people coming into the office and sitting on video calls all day; otherwise, what's the point? ... Work should be fun," she says, underscoring that the court helped make the office a place employees *wanted* to be.

Another reason pickleball excels at team-building is that it creates a level playing field among colleagues. In a single lunchtime tournament, you might see interns scoring points against directors, or accountants teaming up with creatives. Because the game is new to most people, everyone improves together and cheers each other on. The informality of the pickleball court can dissolve the formality of job titles. Companies have capitalized on this by organizing cross-departmental pickleball mixers. For instance, one corporate tournament randomly assigned partners from different divisions, leading to unlikely duos and plenty of good-natured banter. Employees report that these initiatives lead to stronger teams and better communication back at work. A Room & Board employee, Debbie Hutson, shared that initially it was challenging to meet colleagues outside her immediate team – until office pickleball "changed all that," she says. After picking up the game at work, she began interacting with coworkers from all corners of the company. "Now, I'm teaching other employees I normally wouldn't cross paths with how to play pickleball," Hutson notes, adding, "It's helped me build stronger relationships at work, for sure". Stories like this illustrate how a simple game can bridge gaps between departments and create a more cohesive, friendly company culture.

Forward-looking firms also appreciate that pickleball can drive a broader wellness movement. It's not just about exercise (though the health benefits are real); it's about reimagining the workplace as a community space. TIAA's campus redesign, for example, treats outdoor activity as part of the workday, not separate from it. When employees see their leaders prioritizing wellness infrastructure – whether it's pickleball courts, walking trails, or fitness centers – they feel permission to prioritize their own health too. This can translate to lower stress, improved fitness, and reduced burnout. Even tech giants have taken note: companies like Microsoft, Google, and Walmart have added pickleball courts to their campuses as part of creating vibrant, amenity-rich workplaces. The reasoning is clear: a quick doubles match can refresh the mind better than a cup of coffee, and a little friendly competition can make the office feel less like a grind. In summary, pickleball's ease of entry, time-friendly format, and social nature make it a perfect fit for corporate wellness and team-building programs. By investing in play, companies are investing in healthier, happier, and more connected employees.

6.2: Case Studies – Leaders Who Play

Pickleball isn't just being embraced by companies at the organizational level; it's also capturing the hearts of CEOs, entrepreneurs, and business leaders who play the game themselves. In this section, we highlight a few inspiring anecdotes of leaders who have found that pickleball benefits their professional lives – from networking and dealmaking to personal wellness and team leadership. These case studies, some real and some composite for illustration, reinforce that pickleball isn't "just a game" for these leaders, but a catalyst for positive change in how they network, manage, and lead.

Consider the example of a tech startup CEO – let's call him Alex – who was looking for a way to cultivate stronger relationships with partners and investors. Alex had tried the usual networking circuit (coffee meetings, cocktail mixers) but found them somewhat stiff and transactional. A longtime tennis player, he discovered pickleball through colleagues and had a lightbulb moment: why not invite business contacts to play? He started organizing weekly pickleball meetups on Thursday evenings, inviting a rotating mix of venture capitalists, potential clients, and fellow entrepreneurs. What began as three people hitting around grew into a regular meetup dubbed "Tech Pickleball," drawing dozens of professionals. This fictionalized scenario mirrors real life – in Brooklyn, for instance, entrepreneur John Diloreto started hosting *Tech Pickleball* sessions on Friday mornings, which grew from 3 people to over 50 attendees each week. They provided coffee, bagels, and paddles; participants provided the energy. Diloreto found that playing together allowed people to "build an authentic connection by sharing in a game," instead of the forced small talk of typical networking events. The outcome? New business for his AI company, introductions to venture capital firms, and even a few people landing new jobs – all traced back to bonds formed on the pickleball court. Alex's experience was similar: over a few months of pickleball meetups, he not only got much-needed exercise but also forged genuine friendships with investors. Those friendships paved the way for honest business conversations in a low-pressure setting. In one case, a casual post-game chat about industry challenges led to a partnership idea that later became a signed deal. For leaders like Alex, pickleball became the *next big networking platform* – more inclusive and fun than the golf course, and more engaging than a conference happy hour.

Some high-profile business figures are so bullish on pickleball's potential that they're literally investing in the sport. It's not just athletes and celebrities buying Major League Pickleball (MLP) teams – the ownership ranks now include prominent entrepreneurs and executives. For example, an "absurdly star-studded" group of investors in MLP features Mavericks owner Mark Cuban and VaynerMedia CEO Gary Vaynerchuk alongside sports legends. When figures like Cuban and

Vaynerchuk put their money into a professional pickleball franchise, it signals that they view the sport as more than a pastime. They see a platform for community, networking, and growth. As one MLP investor put it, there's a rush to be part of "America's next big sport" – one that is far more accessible to the masses than, say, owning a piece of an NFL team. These business leaders recognize that pickleball's rapid rise has created opportunities to connect with a diverse audience of fans and players. In fact, many MLP investors actively play the game and mingle at events, finding it a refreshing way to meet other leaders on equal footing (after all, on the court, a CEO has to follow the same rules as everyone else!).

Leaders inside organizations are also championing pickleball to improve workplace culture. We saw how Room & Board's HR leadership used the company's pickleball court to boost morale. Nancy Manley, the Chief People Officer, observed dozens of employees taking up pickleball and embraced it as a well-being initiative. "To have happy, healthy, and productive employees, you need to give them the space and tools to take care of themselves," Manley says. "Pickleball is just another outlet for people to destress and sweat a little". This quote embodies a progressive leadership philosophy: the best leaders don't just push for productivity at all costs – they encourage play and self-care, understanding it leads to more sustainable success. By picking up a paddle herself and advocating for playtime during work, a leader like Manley sets a tone that balance is valued. The effects are tangible: employees feel more energized and loyal to a company that invests in their well-being. One young manager at Room & Board noted that having the chance to play at the office "changed everything" in terms of meeting colleagues beyond her own team. She went from struggling to network internally to being at the center of an interdepartmental pickleball crew, where she even found herself teaching others the game. The stronger inter-department relationships that resulted weren't an accidental side effect – they were the direct outcome of a leadership team willing to try something unconventional for team-building.

We also have examples of leaders using pickleball explicitly as a tool for their professional edge. A sales director at a finance firm (let's call her Maria for our composite case) started inviting top clients to play pickleball as a way to deepen relationships. Maria had read that many professionals find pickleball more efficient for networking than golf – you can play multiple short games in the time it takes to do 18 holes, and it doesn't demand a high skill level to enjoy. Initially, some colleagues were skeptical: would clients be interested? It turned out many were not only interested but enthusiastic; some had even been looking for an excuse to try the sport. Maria organized a quarterly "picklebiz" morning where a few team members and clients met at a local court. The atmosphere was relaxed – business suits swapped for polo shirts and sneakers – and they'd play friendly round-robins for an hour. One of Maria's clients, the CEO of a small tech company, later remarked that seeing her on the court, cheering and laughing, made him *trust* her more in business: "It was like I got to know the real you, not just the sales rep," he told her. In one instance, Maria recounted a story that has since become legend at her firm: *"We signed our biggest contract of the quarter after a morning on the pickleball court – the relaxed environment helped both sides open up,"* she revealed. Whether entirely true or a bit embellished, that anecdote has inspired many of Maria's colleagues (including some senior VPs) to dust off their sneakers and join the next pickleball outing.

Even entrepreneurs outside corporate walls are leveraging pickleball to build community and ideas. In Pittsburgh, startup founder Kit Mueller launched a weekly founders-and-investors pickleball meetup called "Dinks and Deals." His vision was to bring together people who might fund or found the next big company in a setting free of conference rooms and pitch decks. The weekly gathering at a local park started small but gained momentum, drawing around 10 people regularly and forging new friendships. One participant, the CEO of a growing sustainability startup, said playing each week kept her connected to the community: "Meeting some good people and getting a good workout in before the rest of my day is just a plus," she noted. These stories highlight a trend: leaders are not only playing pickleball for fun, they're strategically integrating it into their leadership style and networking habits. From improving approachability (a CEO who will rally on the court might be seen as more down-to-earth by employees) to expanding one's network (you never know who you'll meet at open play), pickleball is proving to be a catalyst for professional growth. In essence, these leaders who play are finding that the court is an extension of the boardroom – a place where relationships are built, ideas are exchanged, and even deals are sparked, all under the guise of play.

6.3: Closing Deals and Client Networking

If golf was the traditional sport of business networking in the 20th century, pickleball is fast becoming its 21st-century successor. This section zeroes in on how professionals are using pickleball as a tool for client entertainment and deal-making. The appeal is straightforward: pickleball provides a fresh, less formal way to bond with business partners, offering all the networking upside of golf with fewer barriers to entry. Here, we'll discuss practical tips for leveraging pickleball in business settings, share etiquette advice, and illustrate how a friendly game can break down barriers that might otherwise stall a negotiation.

Turning Play into Networking Opportunities: Much like scheduling a golf outing or a client dinner, savvy professionals are incorporating pickleball into their relationship-building toolkit. Here are a few practical ideas:

- **Host a Pickleball Clinic at Conferences:** Next time you're organizing or attending a conference, consider adding a pickleball clinic or mini-tournament to the agenda. Instead of the typical cocktail hour, attendees can hit the courts for some casual games. It's an excellent ice-breaker – people chat between points and cheer each other on, creating a shared memory. If many are new to the game, hire a local coach or an experienced player to run a quick clinic so everyone feels included. The novelty of a "conference pickleball outing" is often a draw in itself, attracting a mix of participants.

- **Invite Clients for a Friendly Game:** Instead of defaulting to a fancy dinner or golf outing, invite a potential client or business partner to join you for a pickleball match. The cost is minimal (often just reserving a public court or club time, and maybe providing spare paddles and balls) and the time commitment is flexible. A morning game followed by coffee, or an early evening match before a casual meal, can be more engaging than sitting across a table in a formal setting. Importantly, pickleball's doubles format means you can include more people – for example, a couple of folks from your team and a couple from the client's team can all play together, mixing sides. This creates a collaborative environment rather than an "us vs. them" dynamic.

- **Sponsor or Join a Charity Pickleball Event:** Charity golf tournaments have long been a staple of corporate philanthropy and networking. Now, charity pickleball events are emerging as trendy alternatives. By sponsoring a local pickleball fundraiser (or organizing one), companies can do good for the community while rubbing shoulders with other local business leaders and officials in a relaxed atmosphere. Playing for a common cause tends to put everyone in a positive mood, and it showcases your company's community spirit. Plus, these events often draw a diverse crowd – including those who might not golf – expanding your reach. Bringing clients or prospects to a charity pickleball event is a triple win: you bond over a fun activity, support a cause, and get introduced to a wider network of professionals.

Why It Works: Evidence is mounting that these approaches are effective. Executives report that pickleball can be a more efficient networking tool than golf in several ways. For one, it's *inclusive and easy.* The game can be enjoyed by beginners within minutes, unlike golf which may intimidate novices. This means you can comfortably invite a broad range of people – regardless of age, gender, or athletic background – and everyone will be able to participate and have fun. Additionally, the shorter game time means you can interact with more people in a session. A morning at the pickleball courts might allow you to play with 6–8 different partners or opponents as you rotate, whereas a round of golf typically limits you to one foursome (the same 3 other people) for several hours. As one Reddit user quipped, pickleball is like the "speed dating" of business sports – you can meet 40 people in a day, whereas with golf, meeting 8 would be a lot. The Pickleball Club of Tysons summarized this well: companies see a greater return on investment with pickleball, as it "allows for more interaction within a shorter timeframe and at a lower cost compared to golf". Simply put, you can achieve a lot of quality networking in a brief period, without the hefty greens fees or an all-day commitment.

Moreover, pickleball tends to foster a *different tone* of interaction. The environment is inherently more lighthearted and less formal than many traditional client-entertainment settings. You're in athletic gear, not business attire. Everyone is a bit more relaxed, maybe even a little vulnerable (especially if they're new to the game and might swing and miss a few shots). This shared humility can break down hierarchies – titles and negotiations take a backseat to the immediate fun and challenge of the game. One Bloomberg report noted that pickleball offers a "less formal, more engaging environment, fostering camaraderie and breaking down barriers among participants". People tend to drop their guard when they're laughing over a missed serve or high-fiving a great rally. That camaraderie can carry over when you eventually sit down at the negotiating table – it's easier to find common ground or resolve a sticking point with someone you've enjoyed a game with. A life coach interviewed about using pickleball for client interactions mentioned that the sport was a *refreshing alternative* to stuffy meetings, helping her clients (especially those who might be uncomfortable in traditional corporate settings) loosen up and connect more authentically.

Etiquette and Approach: When using pickleball for business networking or deal-making, it's important to handle it with the right touch. The goal isn't to win at all costs, but to ensure everyone has a good time. Here are a few etiquette tips and best practices:

- *Gauge the Competitive Tone:* If your client or partner is brand new to pickleball, consider playing cooperatively or mixing teams (each side having a mix of company/client players) rather than an us-versus-them match that could become overly competitive. If everyone is of similar skill and enjoys competition, a friendly tournament-style game can be fun – just keep it light. Avoid running up the score or smashing balls at a beginner; this is about relationship-building, not the club championship.

- *Provide Gear and Guidance:* If you're inviting others, bring extra paddles and balls. Make it as easy as possible for them to say yes

– maybe suggest, "Don't worry if you haven't played, we have spare equipment and I'll explain the basics." You could even start with a quick demo or warm-up rally to get everyone comfortable. Ensure that no one feels left out or embarrassed by their level of play.

- *Focus on Fun and Interaction:* Remember, the *point* of the outing is the interaction, not the game itself. Use the time between points or games to chat about non-work topics – families, hobbies, the absurdity of how you missed that last shot – to deepen personal rapport. Compliment good shots generously, and laugh off the mistakes. If the conversation veers toward business naturally, that's fine, but often it's best to let the relationship strengthen organically on the court and save the serious business talk for afterwards (perhaps over a casual lunch or coffee).

- *Be Mindful of Inclusion:* If you're hosting a larger networking pickleball event, make sure to shuffle players so that cliques don't form. Introduce people to each other. As the host, your role is part facilitator, part player. Also, consider accessibility – pickleball is low-impact, but if someone has physical limitations, you can adapt by playing half-court or one-on-one in the kitchen (non-volley) area only. The key is to ensure everyone, regardless of ability, feels involved and enjoys the experience.

By following these guidelines, you set the stage for the pickleball outing to be remembered positively – as a unique and enjoyable encounter rather than an awkward or overly competitive one.

The true power of pickleball in closing deals lies in the *shared experience* it creates. When you've run around the court with someone, exchanged smiles or good-natured trash talk, you've built a bit of a bond. That bond can translate into business trust. Two executives who might struggle to break the ice in a formal meeting can find themselves joking like old friends after a game. We heard earlier the (fictional but plausible) testimonial of a team signing its biggest contract following a pickleball session – the relaxed environment let both sides open up and discover mutual trust. There's also the efficiency factor: as one networking expert pointed out, a pickleball session is usually only 2–3 hours at most, and you're not stuck talking to the same person the whole time. It's social and fluid; you can rotate partners, or chat with spectators on the bench during breaks. This fluidity means networking happens naturally. In one real-life example, a communications VP met a retired executive during a local pickleball community play and learned she'd been at the very company the VP had been hoping to pitch – a connection she might never have made in a typical networking event. Stories like this underscore how pickleball can serendipitously put the right people in your path.

Finally, let's not underestimate the *cost advantage* in closing deals on the court. A few hours of court rental (often free at public parks or modest at indoor clubs) and maybe some cold drinks afterwards are all it takes – a far cry from expensive client dinners or golf outings that involve travel, fees, and lost work time. This lower cost means a higher ROI when a deal does result. And even when a deal isn't immediately on the table, you've still invested in the relationship at a bargain price. It's no wonder, then, that companies are increasingly ditching golf for pickleball to get deals done. They're finding that it's not only friendlier on the budget, but can also reach a broader, more diverse group of clients. Golf has traditionally skewed towards a certain demographic, whereas pickleball's mass appeal extends across ages and genders. One corporate report noted that some executives have turned to pickleball to engage clients who wouldn't be as comfortable on the golf course, thereby reaching a more diverse audience. In summary, by integrating a bit of play into their deal-making process, professionals are discovering they can create stronger bonds, have more meaningful interactions, and ultimately drive business success – all while having a good time.

6.4: Integrating Play into a Busy Schedule

With all these benefits on the table – improved wellness, better team cohesion, networking opportunities, and even closing deals – many busy professionals might still ask: *This sounds great, but how on earth do I fit pickleball into my packed schedule?* Indeed, integrating play into an already busy life can seem challenging. This section offers practical strategies to weave pickleball into your routine, no matter how packed your calendar. The underlying message is empowering: making room for play can actually enhance your productivity and success, rather than detract from it.

Schedule it like a meeting: The first strategy is simple but powerful – treat your pickleball time as you would an important meeting or appointment. If you live by your calendar, actually block out a slot for pickleball. Some companies have made this incredibly easy: at Room & Board, for example, employees can reserve the office pickleball court using the same Outlook system they use to book conference rooms. It sends a clear signal that playing is an accepted (even encouraged) part of the day. While not every office has an on-site court, you can still take a page from this approach. Perhaps you set a recurring "Wednesday 7:00 AM Pickleball" on your calendar and treat it as inviolable. A number of executive teams have started doing just that – forming an informal club that meets once a week at a local court, bright and early before the workday chaos begins. They find it's a great way to network internally and externally. In one real instance, the *Tech Pickleball* group in Brooklyn meets every Friday at 7:30 AM, and dozens of professionals show up consistently. By having that standing appointment, it becomes a habit. Participants plan around it, the same way they'd plan around a weekly staff meeting. If your company supports it, you might even reserve a regular slot in a nearby gym or community center as a "company pickleball hour" where colleagues know they can drop in. The key is to give play the priority it deserves – if you only play when you have free time, you'll never play, because whoever has free time? Instead, allocate time to play and arrange other tasks around it. Think of it as an investment in your effectiveness; a mid-week game can recharge you much like a vacation day would, but in miniature.

Start small and build momentum: For those still skeptical or extremely tight on time, start with baby steps. You don't need to commit to a two-hour block right away. Even a 30-minute session can be beneficial. Perhaps you step out during an extended lunch break for a quick solo practice (many parks have walls or machines you can hit against), or you play one fast game to 11 points with a coworker after work. One Room & Board employee, Liz Martin, often squeezes in an hour on the court *before* her meetings begin. She only picked up pickleball recently, but it rapidly became one of her favorite parts of the day. Why? Because she noticed that even 30 minutes of play had tangible effects: "I feel sharper, I feel more awake," she reported on returning to her desk. That boost in productivity and alertness can more than make up for the time spent playing. In fact, some companies are rethinking the whole concept of breaks and recess for adults. Rather than seeing a mid-day game as "time lost," they see it as "time gained" in terms of employee energy and focus. If you're a manager, you might encourage your team to have a weekly pickleball break and see if it elevates their mood and output in the afternoon. If you're an executive, consider delegating a non-essential meeting or two and using that slot for physical activity – you might find you return to work with clearer decision-making abilities. There's a reason many top leaders, from CEOs to U.S. presidents, schedule daily exercise: it's a force multiplier for their productivity. Pickleball, with its mix of physical activity and social fun, can be an especially effective way to reset your brain during a busy week.

Leverage weekends and travel opportunities: Not all networking or team-building has to happen Monday to Friday. Many professionals are taking advantage of weekends to combine leisure with career benefits. Local pickleball clubs and city leagues often have weekend drop-in sessions or mixers. These are typically casual gatherings where anyone can show up and get matched for games. It's an excellent chance to meet people outside your usual circle – you might find yourself playing with a local business owner, a potential client, or someone who becomes a mentor or friend. One Fortune 500 executive shared that he started attending a Saturday community pickleball meetup purely to relax, and ended up befriending a few other executives and community leaders there, broadening his network in a genuine way. So, if weekdays truly don't permit any play, look to a Saturday morning as a personal playtime. It doubles as stress relief and informal networking.

For the road warriors among us – those who travel frequently for business – pickleball can travel with you. Before your next trip, consider looking up if your destination has pickleball courts or clubs (the growing popularity of the sport means many hotels, resorts, and public parks now feature courts, and apps/websites can help locate them). Packing a pair of athletic shoes and even a collapsible paddle in your carry-on can open up the possibility of a game on the road. Some salespeople have even started inviting out-of-town clients to a pickleball game when visiting – a welcome change from the usual dinner routine. And if clients are unavailable, you can still drop into a local open-play session for a dose of exercise and perhaps meet other traveling professionals doing the same thing. It's networking, fitness, and sightseeing all in one – playing in a new city's pickleball scene can give you a fun story to share back home or in your next meeting ("You won't believe it, but I played pickleball with a group of retired NASA engineers in Florida last week…").

Make it non-negotiable (within reason): Executives at the highest levels often have schedules booked back-to-back. Yet, some have managed to integrate play by treating it as a non-negotiable appointment with themselves. It might be a CEO who blocks out every Tuesday at 5

PM for "personal training" which occasionally is a pickleball game with a coach or friend, or a partner at a law firm who comes in a bit later twice a week after hitting the courts at dawn. The trick is to shift mindset: rather than viewing play as the thing you do after *everything* else is done (which, in a busy job, is never), view it as part of your job of being an effective leader. Taking care of your physical health and mental well-being through enjoyable exercise is as important as answering emails – perhaps more so, because a healthy, happy professional will answer emails more efficiently and creatively. One CFO described how making time for pickleball actually forced him to delegate more – and he discovered his team rose to the occasion. By stepping away for his standing game, he empowered a junior colleague to lead a routine meeting, which became a growth opportunity for that person. In other words, integrating play can have positive ripple effects on your leadership and team development.

Hacks and tips: If you need a few extra hacks to make pickleball part of your life, consider these. Keep a pickleball bag in your car or office with a change of clothes, a paddle, balls, and a water bottle – being prepared removes one more barrier to a spontaneous game. Use scheduling tools or apps: if your workplace is like Room & Board's, set up a court reservation system or even a simple email list where interested coworkers can coordinate games. This way, you don't spend time in back-and-forth coordination; people can easily see when courts are free or who's up for playing. Also, mix business with pleasure deliberately by inviting work contacts to join you recreationally. For example, if you know a colleague from another department also plays, make it a point to schedule a regular game together – it doubles as inter-department networking and breaks the silo between your teams. If you're mentoring someone, consider doing your catch-up chat while hitting on the court rather than in an office. Sometimes conversation flows more freely when people are engaged in an activity side by side.

To wrap up, the overarching idea is to be intentional about play. We often schedule every minute of our workday but leave leisure to whatever scraps of time remain. By flipping that script – or at least penciling leisure onto the calendar – you ensure it doesn't get perpetually postponed. The returns on investing time in pickleball (or any enjoyable physical activity) are well worth it. You'll likely see improvements in your health, from cardiovascular fitness to weight management, which in turn reduces stress and sick days. Your mental clarity will thank you – many players report coming off the court with a clearer mind and elevated mood, perfectly primed to tackle complex problems at work. One employee attested that after playing, "I feel sharper, more awake," and noticed heightened productivity when she returned to her desk. Additionally, you'll accumulate social capital: new contacts, whether they're simply friends who enrich your life or professional connections that could open doors. The weekly pickleball gathering we mentioned earlier not only kept participants fit but directly resulted in business opportunities and even job leads for some. It's networking without the name tag – relationship-building while doing something genuinely fun.

In conclusion, integrating pickleball into a busy schedule is a matter of prioritization and creativity. By scheduling play, starting small, utilizing weekends/travel, and treating it as a vital appointment, professionals can make room for this high-return activity. The irony is that dedicating time to play can make you *better* at your work: healthier, happier, more connected, and more energized. It turns out that a bit of time on the court can pay dividends in the boardroom – a win-win scenario for both career and personal well-being. So grab that paddle, mark your calendar, and get ready to see your hobby become your secret weapon for success. As this chapter has shown, the journey from court to boardroom is not only possible; it's already happening in forward-thinking circles – and you can be part of it. Game on!

Chapter 7

Game Plan – Getting Started and Succeeding in Pickleball as a Busy Professional

In this closing chapter, we turn theory into action. Now that you know why pickleball is such a powerful outlet for fitness, networking, and fun, it's time to learn how to weave it into your busy life. Consider this your practical guide to starting (or elevating) your pickleball journey while balancing a demanding career. We'll cover the essentials – from finding a court and gearing up, to improving your game and maximizing benefits on a tight schedule. Throughout, the tone is encouraging and actionable. By the end, you should feel confident about picking up a paddle and reaping *The Pickleball Advantage* for yourself. Let's dive in!

7.1: Finding Your Court and Community

First things first: how and where do you play? The good news is that pickleball courts are popping up everywhere. In fact, the number of places to play in the U.S. has exploded – growing by over 50% in the last year alone to more than 16,000 locations nationwide. Public parks are painting pickleball lines on old tennis courts, community centers are scheduling open play hours, gyms are adding courts, and private clubs are investing in pickleball facilities. With so many venues, you're likely closer than you think to your first game.

Finding a court is easier than ever. You can start with USA Pickleball's official court finder (now powered by Pickleheads), which lets you search for courts and playing groups in your area. Simply enter your city or ZIP code, and you'll discover nearby options – whether it's a dedicated pickleball complex or a few shared-use courts at a local park. According to USA Pickleball, this database (maintained with the help of thousands of local ambassadors) is the most reliable, up-to-date listing of courts and schedules. In other words, wherever you are, a pickleball game is likely just a click away.

Beyond official tools, don't overlook community-driven resources. Local Facebook groups and apps often connect pickleball enthusiasts to organize games. Many beginners find it comfortable to seek out others at their skill level online – for example, new players often "lurk" in Facebook groups and jump in when someone posts about beginner meet-ups. Try searching your city name plus "pickleball" on social media – chances are you'll find a group coordinating casual play, beginner clinics, or league nights. Apps like Meetup or TeamReach also have pickleball groups where you can RSVP for open play sessions. These online communities are typically very welcoming to newcomers.

If you prefer a more old-fashioned approach, head to your local park or rec center and check the bulletin boards or posted schedules. Many parks have adopted a paddle rack system: you place your paddle in line to rotate into a game. Don't be intimidated if you see a mix of ages and skill levels – pickleball culture is famously friendly and inclusive. Even if you show up alone, players will invite you to join a doubles game. And if courts are busy, use the chance to observe and soak up pointers. Remember, every pickleball player was a beginner once, and most are happy to help newcomers learn the ropes.

For the truly time-crunched executive, consider bringing pickleball right to your doorstep. Some busy professionals are starting workplace pickleball groups to squeeze in games without leaving the office. All it takes is a flat space (like a parking lot or an empty warehouse floor) and a portable net. Imagine a quick 30-minute pickleball match in the company parking lot during lunch or a Friday afternoon round-robin as a team-bonding activity. Even a makeshift setup can work for a casual game – many portable nets are easy to set up and take down. If your workplace has an employee wellness committee, pitch the idea of a pickleball net in the vicinity. It's a fun way to get colleagues moving and interacting beyond the conference room. Some companies have even gone further: CityPickle, a New York-based pickleball facility, reported they receive 25+ corporate event requests *per day* from groups wanting to play – a sign that corporate America is embracing pickleball for team building and client outings. You might spark the next trend at your office!

As you venture out, keep in mind the importance of community. Pickleball isn't just about the court; it's about the people. Joining a beginner-friendly league or attending open-play sessions can accelerate your learning *and* expand your network of partners. Many city leagues have novice divisions where everyone is new, so no one cares if you mess up the score or hit the ball out – you're all learning together. Community centers often run weekly beginner nights or even offer a first lesson free to encourage participation. For example, the Pikes Peak Pickleball Association in Colorado runs regular beginner lessons and round-robins for players rated 2.0 and up (basically novices), ensuring there's a gentle on-ramp for new players. One club in Utah even ran a "Three for Free" promotion: one free intro lesson and two free open-play passes for beginners to meet people and get hooked on the game. These welcoming initiatives remove the intimidation factor and prove that accessible options exist for every schedule and budget.

Bottom line: you do not have to go it alone. There's a vast pickleball network ready to embrace you, whether you're a total novice or dusting off skills from your youth. By tapping into local courts and communities, you'll seamlessly integrate into the pickleball scene. And you might be surprised how quickly it happens – mention to a few friends or colleagues that you're interested, and you'll likely hear, *"Oh, I play too! Let's go this weekend."* There's a saying that *anytime you mention pickleball, it instantly builds your network*, and it's true. The sport's social nature is a feature, not a bug. In fact, many enthusiasts say the friendships formed on the court are the biggest win. As one pickleball-playing attorney confessed, *"For me, the most important benefits of playing pickleball are meeting new friends and simply having fun!"*. Keep that spirit in mind as you find your court and your community – you're not just learning a game, you're gaining a joyful new circle of connections.

7.2: Gearing Up – What You Need (and Don't)

One of the beautiful things about pickleball is its simplicity – you don't need an expensive set of golf clubs, a truckload of gear, or a country club membership to start. In this section, we'll outline the basic equipment you need (and what you *don't* need) to hit the ground running.

Pickleball Paddle: The paddle is your primary tool, but it doesn't have to break the bank. A mid-range composite paddle will serve you perfectly well as a beginner. Look for something in the $50–$100 range from a reputable brand – these paddles typically have a lightweight polymer core and a fiberglass or graphite face, offering a good balance of power and control for newbies. Don't get overwhelmed by the dizzying array of paddle technology on the market. Yes, there are paddles with high-tech cores and textured carbon fiber faces that pros use, but you can worry about those nuances later (if ever). In fact, many community centers have loaner paddles or starter sets; you might borrow a paddle for your first few games to get a feel. Affordable options abound – basic wood paddles can cost as little as $15, and decent entry-level composite paddles often go for under $50. (As a point of reference, pickleball paddles can be as cheap as $20 in sporting goods stores.) The key is to get a paddle that feels comfortable in your hand. Standard weight is around 7-8 ounces; lighter paddles are easier to maneuver, heavier ones can add power – but we're splitting hairs. Any mid-range paddle is fine to start. Over time, you might demo a friend's paddle and develop personal preferences (grip thickness, weight, material), but there's truly no need to overspend as a beginner.

Balls: Pickleballs themselves are inexpensive (usually a few dollars each) and come in indoor and outdoor varieties. What's the difference? Mainly the number and size of holes. Indoor balls have larger holes (usually 26 holes) and are made of a slightly softer, lighter plastic. They're designed for control in wind-free environments like gyms. Outdoor balls have smaller holes (40 holes) and are made of harder plastic, a bit heavier to resist wind. If you're mostly playing outdoors (which many folks do), grab a pack of outdoor pickleballs – the classic bright yellow ones are popular for visibility. If you play indoors on a basketball court surface, you'll want indoor balls which are easier to control and don't skid as much. That said, as a new player you don't need to obsess over ball types; use whatever is provided or whatever others are using at the court. Most open-play groups supply a few balls for everyone to use. Just know that if you buy your own, match the ball to the environment (and don't worry, the packaging will clearly say "indoor" or "outdoor").

Footwear: Invest in a good pair of court shoes – this is one area not to skimp on. By "court shoes," we mean tennis, pickleball, or volleyball shoes with supportive soles designed for quick lateral movements. These sports involve a lot of side-to-side shuffling and pivoting, so the shoes have flatter, grippier soles and lateral support to protect your ankles. Running shoes, by contrast, are built for forward motion and cushioning, not sudden stops or cuts; wearing running shoes on a pickleball court is a common culprit for rolled ankles. Experts strongly advise using proper court footwear: *"Court shoes are best for pickleball. They support your ankles and feet as you turn and pivot. Avoid running shoes.".* If you already have tennis shoes, those will work perfectly. Ensure they fit well and haven't lost their tread. Good court shoes will help you move confidently and prevent injury, especially as you get used to the footwork.

Apparel: Here, anything comfortable and weather-appropriate will do. There's no strict dress code in pickleball – wear the same athletic attire you might wear to the gym or a casual tennis hit. In warm weather, shorts or lightweight joggers and a moisture-wicking t-shirt work well; in cooler weather, you might opt for layers like leggings and a light jacket you can peel off as you warm up. Some players like to wear a cap or visor and sunglasses for sun protection outdoors. Since games are quick and there's a lot of starting/stopping, having breathable fabrics helps. Also consider bringing along a small towel and a water bottle. Hydration is important, as with any exercise. Make sure to drink enough water before and during play – you'll perform better and recover faster if you stay hydrated. A sports water bottle that you can refill courtside is a great accessory (and far cheaper than a post-game trip to urgent care for heat exhaustion!).

That's really it – paddle, ball, shoes, comfortable clothes, water. It's refreshingly simple. You might notice some players with extra gear: fancy neoprene paddle covers, gloves, eye protection goggles, hats with pickleball slogans, etc. Feel free to ignore the extras until you've got a few games under your belt. The only other thing you may consider early on is safety gear if needed: for instance, if you have sensitive knees, an elastic knee brace or sleeve can provide support; some older competitors swear by a little wrist brace or compression sleeve. These are purely optional and based on personal comfort.

Before you jump into play, let's touch on a few preventive measures to keep you playing strong. Pickleball is low-impact and accessible, but it's still exercise, so treating it like a sport will help you avoid injuries. Warm up for 3–5 minutes with light activity before your first game: for example, brisk walking, gentle jogging in place, or some dynamic stretches for your legs and shoulders. Sports medicine experts recommend getting your blood flowing and then stretching major muscle groups before you start intense play. This reduces the risk of muscle pulls and gives your body a chance to prep for those quick bursts of movement. Likewise, after you finish playing, do a short cool down (slow walk, easy stretching) to let your heart rate come down gradually and ward off stiffness. These simple steps – a brief warm-up, a post-game stretch – are often skipped by eager new players, but they can save you a lot of soreness. Think of it as an investment in your ability to play again tomorrow!

Another crucial tip: listen to your body. As a busy professional, you might be tempted to squeeze in pickleball whenever possible, but avoid the trap of overdoing it right away. It's okay to start with one or two sessions a week and ramp up. If you experience pain (beyond normal muscle soreness), take a rest day or two. *Don't play through serious pain.* Pickleball is addictive, but rest and recovery are part of any fitness routine. As one physical therapist advises, you should give your body time to adapt – if you have sore muscles or joints, use ice and rest until the pain subsides. The game will still be there tomorrow.

In terms of gear hype, you'll quickly notice the pickleball market is booming – there are always "hot" new paddles or shoes being talked about. Our advice: keep it practical. To begin, you truly *can* start with a borrowed paddle or an affordable starter kit. Your focus should be on learning the game and enjoying it, not on whether your paddle has the latest graphite face or your outfit looks pro. As you progress, you might choose to upgrade equipment (and certainly, invest in quality gear if you fall in love with the sport). But it's refreshing that in pickleball, unlike some sports, the barrier to entry is low. One recent business article noted that paddles can be had for under $30 and courts are often free – highlighting that pickleball's low cost of entry is a big part of its appeal for busy professionals who don't want another expensive hobby. You don't need a $500 driver like in golf or a bespoke bicycle – just a paddle, some balls, and willing participants.

To round out this section, let's recap in a quick checklist style:

- **Paddle:** Mid-range composite paddle (borrow or buy ~$50 paddle to start). Don't stress about finding the "perfect" paddle now.

- **Balls:** Outdoor balls (yellow, 40 small holes) for outdoor courts; indoor balls (26 larger holes) for indoor courts. Cheap and often provided at the court.

- **Shoes:** Court shoes with good lateral support. *No running shoes.* Proper footwear protects your ankles and knees.

- **Attire:** Athletic clothes you're comfortable moving in. Dress for the weather/temperature. Hat and sunglasses for sun; layers for cold.

- **Extras:** Water bottle (stay hydrated!), small towel. Optional: sport sunglasses, knee/wrist braces if needed, sweatband, etc.

- **Safety:** 5-minute warm-up and stretching before play; cool-down and stretch after. This prevents common sprains/strains. Listen to your body and rest if needed.

That's all you truly need to get going. Pickleball's beauty is in its simplicity – it doesn't demand much gear or setup, which means you can focus on the fun part right away. As one avid player put it, *"If you have never played pickleball, I encourage you to pick up a paddle and ball, get a good pair of court shoes for support…take a lesson, meet new friends, and have fun playing Pickleball."* In other words: you're prepared, you're equipped, now just get out there and play!

7.3: Maximizing Benefits in Minimal Time

We know our target reader – people like you, ambitious professionals – are short on time. That's one reason you're drawn to pickleball in the first place: it promises a lot of bang for your buck in terms of exercise and networking. This section provides a "cheat sheet" for getting the most benefit (both physical and social) from pickleball when time is at a premium.

Think of this as the busy professional's game plan: how to efficiently use pickleball to stay fit and build connections, without derailing your tight schedule.

Pickleball for Fitness – Quick and Effective

One of the great advantages of pickleball is that even relatively short play sessions can yield meaningful health benefits. You don't need to spend half a day on the court to break a sweat. Research has shown that playing doubles pickleball for even 30 minutes can elevate your heart rate into the moderate-intensity exercise zone sufficient to improve cardiovascular health. In fact, a study of older adults found that more than 70% of their pickleball playing time was spent in moderate to vigorous heart rate zones – meaning the sport naturally gets your blood pumping in a healthful range. Considering the CDC recommends 150 minutes of moderate exercise per week (about 30 minutes, five days a week), a few pickleball sessions can quickly help you meet those guidelines. Two to three hours of play spread across the week and you're there!

For someone with limited time, the key is to maximize intensity and consistency. Here are some tips to get the best workout in minimal time:

- **Play doubles**: Doubles (2 vs 2) is the most common form of pickleball and it's perfect for a moderate cardio workout. An average doubles game will have you moving briskly, but also gives short rests between rallies as either you or your partner hit the ball. Because it's less physically intense than singles (where you cover the whole court), doubles lets you play longer or more frequently without exhaustion, which is ideal for building exercise into your routine. Plus, it's social! If you play doubles for 30–60 minutes, you'll likely accumulate a solid amount of steps and elevated heart rate time. One analysis noted that an hour of doubles play results in roughly 30 minutes of moderate-intensity cardio activity on average. So even a lunch-break pickleball session can count as legitimate exercise toward your weekly goals.

- **Try "pickleball sprints"**: No, this isn't an official term, but think of it as interval training with pickleball. Because games are played to 11 points (and typically last 10–15 minutes), you can structure your play as a series of quick games with short breaks. For example, play a game to 11, take a 2-minute breather, then jump into the next game. Repeat this for a set of 3–4 games. By doing so, you're mimicking a high-intensity interval workout: bursts of activity with brief recovery periods. This can boost your cardiovascular fitness efficiently. If you only have 45 minutes to spare, you might fit in three fast games – that's plenty of movement and probably a lot more fun than running intervals on a treadmill! Pushing yourself a bit during points (hustling for that drop shot, executing a quick volley exchange) will raise your heart rate, and the game's stop-start nature naturally provides interval training. Think of it as cardio with a competitive twist.

- **Focus on continuous play**: When time is limited, try to minimize down-time on the court. That might mean coordinating with your group to rotate efficiently (so there's not a long wait between games) or playing "winners stay on" if others are waiting, so you get to keep moving. If courts are crowded, consider going during off-peak hours when you can play back-to-back games without waiting. Another trick: play half-court singles (also called "skinny singles") with a partner when you can't get a foursome – it's more running for each of you and a great workout in a short time. Essentially, treat your pickleball slot as a focused workout session: arrive on time, warm up quickly, play hard, cool down, and you're done – all within, say, an hour.

- **Leverage mornings or lunchtimes**: Many busy professionals find that early morning pickleball is a golden opportunity. If you can get up a bit earlier, a 7:00 AM game can energize you for the day without eating into work hours. Some communities have organized "sunrise pickleball" groups. For instance, in Brooklyn a group of tech professionals started a 7:30 AM Friday pickleball meet-up and it quickly grew to 50+ regulars who play before heading to the office. They even provide coffee and bagels at the court – talk about multitasking networking, fitness, and breakfast! The takeaway: by 9 AM, those folks have already gotten in a workout and made new connections before most people have finished their first coffee. If mornings aren't your thing, consider a lunchtime session (if you have a flexible break) – a quick game or two can clear your mind and count as exercise. The sport is fast to play, especially compared to something like golf. You can play a complete pickleball match in 15 minutes, whereas golf demands at least 4 hours for 18 holes. This speed and flexibility are a big reason why pickleball is eclipsing golf as the go-to sport for many executives.

Now, what about skill improvement in minimal time? Let's say you can only commit a couple of hours per week – how do you make the most of it to actually get better at the game? The key is intentional practice even within your limited play. Use each game as a learning experience: perhaps dedicate one session to focusing on your serve (try a high, deep serve consistently), another session to practice dinks (the soft shots into the kitchen) with a partner during warm-up. If you can grab a few minutes before games start, do a quick drill or two – for example, rally back and forth with a partner aiming only for the kitchen line to hone your control. Little bits of focused practice, inserted into your play time, will compound improvements without needing separate "drill days." Also, seek feedback from more experienced players in those moments – most are happy to give a pointer or two that can instantly help (like how to hold the paddle for a backhand, or where to stand in doubles). In short, practice smart, not necessarily long.

Pickleball for Networking – Quality Connections on Court

We've established that pickleball is not just exercise, but also a prime networking tool for busy professionals. But how can you maximize those networking benefits when your play time is limited? The answer lies in being intentional about when and how you mix with others on the court.

- **Choose prime networking times**: Identify a location and time where the "movers and shakers" play, and try to make that part of your routine. For example, if you know a popular park near the financial district has an after-work pickleball scene on Wednesdays, aim to drop by then, even if just for an hour.

Regularly playing at a busy time means you'll naturally meet a range of people. You don't have to be extroverted or schmoozy – the gameplay and rotation system will introduce you organically. One corporate VP shared that by showing up weekly to her local community courts, she met all sorts of contacts serendipitously – including a retired Disney executive she ended up chatting with, leading to a professional connection down the line. The key is *show up where others show up.*

- **Rotate partners frequently**: In pickleball open play, it's common to mix and match partners for each new game. Embrace that! Don't always play with the colleague or friend you came with. By switching partners each game, you'll interact with more players. It's perfectly fine (and expected) to say "Good game, shall we mix up teams for the next one?" after finishing a round. Rotating partners not only improves your adaptability on court, but also maximizes the number of people you get to know. Remember, you're not playing with the same four people every time – that's one of pickleball's strengths. In a two-hour open play session, you might play 5 or 6 games with a dozen different people. That's a dozen handshakes and introductions – a dozen more folks who now know you (and maybe what you do for a living, if small talk revealed it). Over a few weeks, those acquaintances can turn into genuine connections.

- **Integrate pickleball into business events**: If you have any say in client outings or team activities, suggest pickleball as an option. Increasingly, companies are ditching golf for pickleball to get deals done, because it's cheaper, faster, and more inclusive. You could invite a client or mentor for a morning game – it's a refreshing change from the usual coffee meeting. Many executives find that a friendly pickleball match breaks the ice far better than a stuffy business lunch. In a game, you see someone's personality, teamwork, and even how they handle wins or losses – all in a lighthearted setting. One tech startup founder started hosting a weekly "Tech Pickleball" meetup for fellow entrepreneurs and investors; what began with 3 people grew to over 600 members, with 50+ showing up every Friday at 7:30 AM, leading to new business deals and even job placements resulting directly from those games. That's networking efficiency! You don't need to create a whole event, but even casually inviting a business contact to join you for a game can strengthen your rapport. It's memorable ("Remember when we played pickleball and you hit that crazy shot?") and sets the stage for a more relaxed business relationship.

- **Leverage pickleball as team building**: If you manage a team or lead people, consider using pickleball as a fun reward or bonding activity. For example, you could institute a "Friday 4 PM Pickleball Happy Hour" (with healthy competition and maybe some refreshments after), or set up an interdepartmental mini-tournament. This doesn't have to consume much time – even an hour of play can boost morale. Companies like Salesforce and Dell have already embraced pickleball in their leadership and wellness programs (Salesforce included it in an executive retreat, and Dell offers on-campus matches as part of executive wellness packages). The reason? It's quick, it's enjoyable, and it levels the playing field between juniors and seniors in a way that traditional outings don't. Even if your team is small, a couple of portable nets in the parking lot and you've got a lively event. As a busy leader, this is a high-ROI activity: minimal time, maximum camaraderie (plus you get your exercise in).

- **Combine learning and socializing**: If you truly have limited free time, you might worry that learning pickleball will detract from your networking focus or vice versa. But you can combine them. For example, join a beginner clinic or class – you'll meet other professionals who are also learning. Or hire a coach for a group lesson with three of your work peers or clients. In that one hour, you're improving your skills *and* strengthening relationships with the others in the group through a shared new experience. It's like killing two birds with one pickle(ball).

To summarize this time-maximization strategy, here's a mini game plan:

- Aim for 2–3 hours of play per week (e.g., three 40-minute sessions). This covers your fitness needs by providing moderate exercise and gives enough exposure to meet others.

- Play smart: interval style (short games, minimal downtime) to get your heart rate up.

- Schedule creatively – early mornings, lunchtimes, or immediately after work – to protect your work schedule.

- Regularly attend a popular open play to network widely; rotate partners and mingle.

- Invite colleagues/clients occasionally to join you for a game, blending networking with play.

- Have a goal for each session, however small (e.g., meet one new person or improve one aspect of your game). This keeps your growth intentional even in limited time.

Even with just a couple of hours a week, you can steadily improve your skills, stay fit, and grow your network – provided you approach pickleball with intention. Remember, it's about working smarter, not longer, both in the office and on the court. And one lovely thing about pickleball is that it doesn't *feel* like work – even a focused, time-efficient session will leave you energized and smiling, rather than drained. As busy achievers, that's exactly what we need: an activity that checks multiple boxes (health, social, stress relief) without feeling like yet another obligation. Pickleball, done right, is efficient joy.

7.4: Bringing Pickleball Principles to Work

As we wrap up, let's step back and look at the bigger picture. By now, you've heard how pickleball can get you in shape and expand your network. But perhaps one of the most valuable aspects of adopting pickleball is the mindset and lessons it imparts – which can carry over into your professional life. In this final section, we reflect on the broader lessons the sport offers and how to apply them off the court. In other words, how can *pickleball make you a better leader, team member, or professional?*

Chances are, your pickleball journey thus far (whether through this book or your own playing) has taught you a few things about adaptability, strategy, collaboration, patience, and even humility. These happen to be qualities that serve us well in the workplace. Let's draw the parallels:

- **Adaptability & Quick Strategy:** In pickleball, you have to adjust your play on the fly against different opponents. One moment you're playing a hard-hitting aggressive team, the next you're against a pair of steady dinkers who slow the game down. To succeed, you quickly read the situation and adapt your strategy – maybe you start dinking more with the soft players or adjust your positioning against power hitters. This ability to analyze and respond is directly applicable to business scenarios. Think about negotiations or competitive business situations: you often start with a game plan, but you must be ready to pivot when the other side throws a curveball. Pickleball sharpens this strategic agility. Former Cisco CEO John Chambers, an avid player, likened pickleball to "a mental sprint — you're reacting, strategizing, and building rapport in real time.". Doesn't that sound like a high-stakes business meeting? The sport trains you to make decisions under pressure in a fluid environment. Take it to work: next time you're in a fast-paced project or facing an unexpected challenge, channel that pickleball mindset – stay light on your feet mentally, and adjust your approach as needed. The more you play, the more second-nature this quick strategic thinking becomes.

- **Teamwork and Collaboration:** If you've played doubles, you know it's all about teamwork. Good doubles partners communicate constantly ("yours!" "mine!"), cover for each other's weaknesses, and set each other up for success (like making an easy setup for your partner to smash). You learn to trust a partner and also to do your part, because two people moving in sync will always outperform two individuals doing their own thing. This directly mirrors effective teamwork in the office. Successful teams capitalize on each member's strengths and have each other's backs. Pickleball shows the power of collaboration in a tangible way – you literally can't win alone; you need your partner. It also teaches leadership and support within a team. Sometimes you take the lead (perhaps you're the stronger player covering more court), other times you play a supporting role (setting up your partner). At work, this translates to stepping up when you have expertise and stepping back to let others shine when they have the lead. Another aspect is communication: in doubles, a brief "got it!" or eye contact to coordinate can make or break the point. Similarly, clear communication in a work team prevents tasks from dropping and fosters harmony. Some CEOs have noticed that playing pickleball with colleagues actually breaks down hierarchical barriers – suddenly *everyone* on the court is just a player, equal and working together, and it humanizes relationships. One tech leader noted that shared physical activity like pickleball helps build authentic trust across ranks. Consider organizing a mixed-level game with your team; you might find your department runs more cohesively Monday to Friday after bonding over pickleball on Saturday.

- **Patience and Focus:** Pickleball rallies can require patience. Think of those long dink exchanges at the net – neither side wants to pop the ball up and make a mistake. You might hit 10, 20 soft shots in a row, waiting for the right moment to attack. This cultivates a mental calmness and focus on the process, not just the outcome. Impatience often leads to errors on the court (smashing a ball that was going out, or trying to force a winner too soon). In the workplace, patience and steady focus are equally virtues. Whether it's negotiating a deal, debugging a complex problem, or navigating a career path, the ability to stay composed and methodical under pressure is key. Pickleball reinforces that taking your time to set up the win – rather than rushing – often yields better results. It's a real-life lesson in strategic patience: sometimes you win a rally not by the flashy shot, but by consistently executing and *waiting* for your opponent to err. Translating that to work, it might mean diligently preparing for a client pitch and addressing all details (rather than hastily throwing something together), or remaining calm in a tense meeting and choosing your moment to speak wisely. The focus you practice in watching that ball and executing your shots carries over – many players report improved concentration at work after playing pickleball regularly, likely because the game trains you to shut out distractions (you can't be thinking about your inbox when a ball is hurtling at you!).

- **Continuous Improvement (Kaizen Mindset):** Pickleball, like any skill, rewards consistent practice and incremental improvements. Maybe this week you're working on getting 80% of your serves in, next week you've set a goal to master a backhand volley. These small gains – improving bit by bit – lead to significant jumps in level over time. It's a great reminder of the value of consistent, incremental improvement. Apply this principle to your professional skills or personal development. Rather than expecting overnight success, you learn to appreciate the journey of getting better step by step. Perhaps practicing pickleball inspires you to similarly practice your public speaking, or coding, or management techniques, a little at a time. You've seen on the court how a 1% improvement each time eventually makes you a formidable player; the same goes for the workplace. This mindset also ties into resilience: in pickleball, if you lose a game, you don't quit – you analyze what went wrong, maybe tweak your strategy, and play again. In business, setbacks are inevitable. The "let's adjust and play the next point" attitude is extremely valuable. In fact, some companies have explicitly drawn these parallels – a few leadership coaches use pickleball analogies like *"resetting the point when things go wrong"* as a metaphor for pivoting after business setbacks. The sport's culture of continuous learning (there's always a new shot to learn or a strategy to try) keeps your brain in a growth mindset, which you can carry into your job.

- **Lightheartedness and Culture:** Perhaps one of pickleball's greatest lessons is *not taking oneself too seriously*. The sport is inherently playful – I mean, it's called pickle-ball! There's laughter on the courts, funny rally moments, and often a communal sense of humor. You'll often see an advanced player happily hit around with beginners and share a joke. This humility and jovial spirit are part of why pickleball communities are so tight-knit. Bringing a bit of that levity into the workplace can do wonders for team culture. Leaders who can laugh at themselves and create an environment where it's okay to have fun tend to have more loyal, motivated teams. Pickleball reminds high-powered individuals (who might be under immense stress normally) to enjoy the game – both the literal game and the "game" of work. A CEO playing doubles with an intern is suddenly just another player; that dynamic can carry back to the office in the form of approachability and camaraderie. According to anecdotal reports, employees who've played pickleball with their bosses often report those bosses feel more approachable and the workplace feels friendlier afterward. It's amazing how a bit of friendly competition and shared laughter can break down walls. So, consider infusing your work life with a pinch of pickleball spirit: celebrate small wins, encourage team play, and maybe keep a paddle in your office as a conversation starter – you might discover fellow picklers among your colleagues!

In essence, pickleball isn't just a break *from* work; it can also be a boost *to* your work. The mental agility, social skills, and positive mindset you cultivate on the court make you a better professional off the court. You might find yourself negotiating a deal and suddenly recognizing, "Ah, this is like a long dink rally – stay patient." Or approaching a team project thinking, "How do I set up my partner (colleague) for success, like in doubles?" These parallels are more than cheesy metaphors; they're real frameworks through which sports teach life skills. It's no coincidence that many top executives are avid pickleball players – they see the sport as a microcosm of strategy, adaptability, and relationship-building. As Tom Cove, CEO of the Sports & Fitness Industry Association, said, *"the pickleball craze is alive and well"* and it's teaching leaders to model adaptability and composure on and off the court.

Finally, let's conclude on an inspiring note. By picking up a paddle, you're not only having fun and getting fit – you're unlocking a new arena for personal growth, mental refreshment, and meaningful connection. This little game with a funny name can enhance your life in serious ways. It offers a balanced blend of competition and community, challenge and cheer. In the grind of a busy professional life, pickleball can be your release valve and your enrichment. It's a place where a CFO might high-five a college student over a great rally, where a normally reserved manager might crack a joke after a flubbed shot. Those experiences ripple outward, creating healthier, happier individuals who bring their best selves to work and home.

That is *The Pickleball Advantage* – a powerful tool busy achievers can leverage for years to come. By integrating the game into your routine, you're investing in a healthier body, a sharper mind, a stronger network, and a lighter spirit. So, as we end this chapter and this book, the call to action is clear: grab that paddle and go play. The court is waiting, and so is your advantage. Game on!

Epilogue

Pickleball began as a quirky backyard invention, but its rise into boardrooms, community centers, and professional circles tells a bigger story. For today's leaders and achievers, the sport has proven to be more than a pastime—it's a catalyst for health, clarity, and connection. Every match offers a reminder that performance doesn't only live behind a desk or inside a quarterly report; it thrives when body, mind, and relationships move in harmony.

On the court, titles dissolve. The CEO rallies alongside the intern, the entrepreneur tests strategy against a retiree, and the busy executive finds focus not in a spreadsheet but in the arc of a ball crossing the net. The lessons learned here—resilience, adaptability, patience, creativity— are the same qualities that drive success in business and life. Pickleball compresses them into a fast-paced, laughter-filled format that both challenges and restores.

Beyond fitness metrics or professional advantages, what endures is the sense of belonging. The game offers an antidote to isolation and a chance to remember that progress is best shared. Friendships are formed, ideas are sparked, and stress is left behind in the kitchen zone with each volley.

The Pickleball Advantage is less about a sport and more about a mindset: growth through play, strength through community, and clarity through movement. For those who carry heavy responsibilities, it offers a lightness that is both rare and necessary.

So, step onto the court. Let the sound of the paddle striking the ball remind you that renewal can come from the simplest of games. And as this movement continues to grow, may every match leave you stronger, sharper, and more connected than before. The future of health, focus, and leadership may just be served on a pickleball court.